The Conspiracy of Good Taste

by

Stefan Szczelkun

Second colour edition 2018

Routine Art Co

Contents

Publishing data

The Conspiracy of Good Taste 2nd edition colour London 2018

New ISBN 9781870736718

Printed by Lightning Source.

Brief Introduction

The main part of *The Conspiracy of Good Taste,* is an examination of three middle-class mediators of taste from the later nineteenth century into the twentieth century: William Morris with his influence on design and poetic expression and as the model of left-wing artistic leadership in the latter part of the nineteenth century; Cecil Sharp because of his key role in promoting a sanitised version of working-class culture through the new national state education system; finally Clough Williams-Ellis who was a leader of the repression of an urban self-build housing movement in the mid twentieth century.

I try to look at the roots of classism in the biographies of the three men, and how they repressed working-class culture, with as much attention to the mechanics of class oppression as I could glean from the sources I found. Although this is a very English history, I assume that similar forces would have to be present in the creation of any modern class society.

There follows a longer introduction in which I recall the key readings, people, events and places through which I came to realise the significance of culture in class oppression and the connections I made to how it had affected my own life as a subaltern artist. The next three chapters tell the detailed story of my protagonists Morris, Sharp and Williams-Ellis.

A further chapter outlines a basic theory of class oppression and goes on to give a summary of the history of good taste as a philosophical discourse. I end with my critique of Pierre Bourdieu's *Distinction* to bring the story of good taste into the late twentieth century.

Middle-class mediators of culture are embedded into our present day cultural institutions. Most of these are run without any transparency or public control by the cultural elite of the British establishment. There can be no end to class inequality and oppression without examining and then dismantling this cultural legacy.

My key sources were: E.P. Thompson's *William Morris: romantic to revolutionary* (1955); Dave Harker's *Fakesong: the manufacture of British folk song - 1700 to the present day* (1985); Dennis Hardy and Colin Ward's, *Arcadia for All: the legacy of a makeshift landscape* (1984). Finally, Howard Caygill's *Art of Judgement* (1989), was my main source for a history of taste through the writings of German and English philosophers. With many thanks to those authors.

Photographs without a credit are by the author.

Introduction

No classless society can arise without a cultural base. It cannot be directed from above, but must arise from a rich renewal of people's social relations. The failure of bureaucratic communism has proven this without doubt. A liberatory culture cannot be planned from above. Leadership will be necessary in the sense of people taking initiatives to organise, but bureaucratic forms could not be central to this process. What I intend to show in this book is that people will tend to evolve such a culture given half a chance. What has happened in practice is that the class society has continually reasserted its dominant values with violent acts, which are dressed in the fine robes of civilization, disguised in placid tones of normality. People's culture has been smothered at birth while those who do the vile deed do it with an air of justified reasonableness.

I have painful insights into the oppression of working-class people from my own history. This is a quality of knowledge that has yet to find adequate recognition in the pantheon of learned sources and yet most of us are motivated and directed, limited or inspired by just such subjective knowledge. What I learned was the central and murderous denial of our intellectual capacity that is at the heartless core of class oppression. By this means, we are, as a class, denied a community of intellectual thought by the denial of access to resources and through repeated stories of our mental incompetence. The dominant culture's values and traditions are seen as embodying an excellence, rationality and taste that is beyond reproach. It is presented as intrinsically and universally superior. The dynamic of class oppression around this hub has denied working-class people full intellectual and cultural development. Many areas of our culture are denied altogether and what remains is often devalued, proscribed and impoverished.

For their part, the owning class oppressors are required to have a large area of her own sensibility shut down, numbed or frozen. Their perception of those below them is of matchstick-people - crudely drawn stereotypes. If this were not so, the human beings who comprise the oppressor class could not direct the vile and endless catalogue of crimes against humanity in the name of daily business and yearly profits. Such unrelenting violence and calumny can only happen day in and day out if there is a deep-seated lack of awareness of the consequences of such actions on human life and dignity. The core necessity of any oppressor conditioning - whether it be white, male, adult, able-bodied or ruling class - is to blot out the humanity of the oppressed.

By good fortune I acquired a powerful insight that both sides of the class equation were damaged by the process of oppression, but the dominating class seems unaware of its own debilitating lack.

In some way oppression generates its own smokescreen. By the start of the twentieth century, Sigmund Freud had understood that early hurt could be repressed into an unconscious existence, which might only be accessed by dreams and free association or 'madness'. At the same time, he realised that the repressed constantly seeks expression, sometimes finding it in perverse, bizarre or antisocial behavior. Wilhelm Reich took this further and indicated how political irrationality resulted from such damage. He envisaged mass people's clinics for psychic healing. Harvey Jackins realised some of Reich's dreams by practically by investigating the place of emotion in the healing of such hurts. Since the Seventies, ordinary people in all occupations self-organised to attempt to re-evaluate their own history and recover occluded areas of thinking in the Re-evaluation Co-counseling communities.

The great bourgeois intellectuals were inevitably moulded by their own subconscious desires. These defined the essential truths about human beings as a reflection of bourgeois self-images. Within this schema the working-class was represented as a fictional object - to be denied an autonomous subjectivity or culture. These great theories or grand narratives came to define the social norm of the dominant culture. Most of us then had to grow up within the classifications thrust on us by these fantasies woven by the literary class.

As I studied the characteristics of the dominant culture, it became clear that one of its most persistent and early features is its general denial of direct emotional expression. The maintenance and reinforcement of this denial is often through cultural forms: everything from the facial expression of the 'stiff upper lip' to the immobile seated audience in theatres which became commonplace at the end of the nineteenth century.

Not only are the hurts of oppression repressed into unconsciousness, numbing huge areas of human intelligence, but large areas of the dominant culture seem to have been elaborated from this basis to disguise the foul structure with extravagant surfaces. The values of this culture of artifice are encoded as 'good taste'.

What I wanted to do was to trace how these values of good taste operated in the mechanisms of oppression. The details of economic exploitation have been well explored. The ways in which culture has been used to dominate us are less well understood.

This book follows the lives of three upper-middle-class men who were influential in the direction of this cultural oppression. All of them were writers: William Morris was a wealthy businessman and a pattern designer; Cecil Sharp was a folk-song collector and an educationalist; Clough Williams-Ellis was an architect and town-planner. These three case studies cover the period from the mid-nineteenth century to the mid-twentieth century. These are just three of the more charismatic figures amongst a mass of professionals and philanthropists who managed to repress and stymie the development of an emergent urban working-class culture in the twentieth century. Their often 'sincere' efforts to contribute to a better world were dwarfed and negated by the undertow of their unconscious class values.

William Morris had taken a medieval vision of rural life and work and relayed it as a utopian goal for every proletarian. These unreal myths were cleverly woven into a tapestry, which denied the value and potential of urban working-class culture. Through his wealth, energy and humanitarian charisma he became an icon as the cultural 'Champion of the People'.

Cecil Sharp focused on song and dance, the means by which a

people celebrates its life. Again, he took a romanticised, cleaned up, censored and edited version of a past rural culture and re-presented it as the ideal for a National English song and dance. He presented these ideas through the burgeoning institutions of mass education. All that did not fit his model of respectability was castigated and denounced. In this way, the least threatening aspects of working-class culture were selected and made into the norms of an ersatz National identity. This manufacturing of a national identity was of course in vogue throughout Europe at the time.

Clough Williams-Ellis was an architect and planner. From this position, he attacked the autonomy and tastelessness of the working-class plotland housing as an eyesore. He used the well-established myth of England as a green and pleasant land to demonise this widespread self-build culture that flourished in the 1920s and 1930s. The autonomous activity was limited by regulations or replaced with large scale planning and development. The state presided over crimes that will only be fully recognised when the destruction of working-class community in the pursuit of profit is outlawed.

These three men are simply representatives of a process of oppression, which continued from the 1880s to the 1980s. A process which blasted the heart of radical modern working-class culture, reducing it to a smouldering ruin which was overrun by cheap and distracting commodities. No culture can be destroyed whilst a people live. For culture arises every moment from peoples' lives. Whilst we are chained to the linear and brutal cash nexus we will be working-class, whatever myths delude us with false identities and diversions. We need to reclaim a contemporary working-class identity, which is free of old stereotypes. We need to rediscover the personal and cultural histories that produced us and find ways to heal ourselves from the terrible legacy of hurt left by class oppression. I can only hope that this book can contribute in a small way to this process.

My criticism is leveled at some of the people who write about the lives of these mediators, as well as at the characters themselves. History rings hollow with the absence of working-class voices. Historians are just as likely to suffer from the blanks and stereotypes of classism as their readers. Although I cannot hope to compete with their scholarship, I feel compelled to offer my own analysis to offset at least partly the distorted image of history that we receive.

This analysis reflects the new possibilities latent in our contemporary world. We have everything we need for a flourishing people's culture. We need to rebuild our confidence in our own language, thinking and values. A process that needs to be cultural and be an integral part of the way we live. A process that requires some people from the broadly defined working-class to accept their vocations as intellectuals, to come to terms with their own history and to shake off the fear which makes them keep their conclusions to themselves.

This requires we thaw out, rather than chill out. Working class people have traditionally valued a person's warmth above their appearance. The directing sense of the new intellectually brilliant working-class culture will not be the cool neon eye of capitalism but may rather be a dynamic and intelligent warmth and human connection.

How This Perception Developed

In 1971, I was in The Scratch Orchestra when it was visiting Newcastle and the Northeast of England for its 'Dealer Concert' series. This experimental music group was defined as 'enthusiasts sharing their resources to make music' and concerts involved up to fifty people from classically-trained musicians to sculptors. The Dealer Concerts became notorious through the local media sensationalising the results of Greg Bright's piece 'Sweet FA'. The papers reported that the well known composer Cornelius Cardew had written four-letter words on toilet paper and they got into the hands of some children that were present.

At about the same time I was preparing my study of basic shelter, later to be published by Unicorn Bookshop in Brighton as *'Survival Scrapbook 1: Shelter'*. Unicorn Bookshop, with the imposing beat poet Bill Butler at the helm, had itself recently been taken to court in one of the rash of obscenity trials at around this time - I think it was for selling *The Little Red Schoolbook*.

We were camping by a river just outside Newcastle near the village of Ovingham. Across the river was a brightly painted settlement of about fifty 'shanty' houses. These intrigued me. They were startlingly different from the normal speculative, council or vernacular housing. Many had evidently grown from inventive adaptations of a wheeled

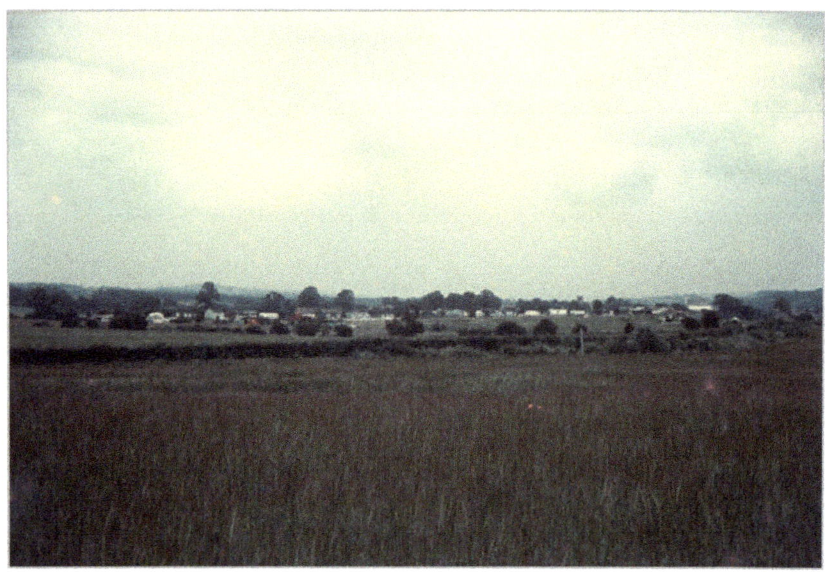

van or shed. Their improvised collage of found or cheap materials had a direct parallel in our activity in the Scratch Orchestra and I took a morning off to photograph them. Later, as I traveled about the country, I discovered more of these shanties in the next few years. They enjoyed a minor architectural vogue at the time and I wrote short articles for the magazines *Architectural Design* and *Radical Technology*, but it was to be almost twenty years before the full implications of my fascination with these structures would become clear to me.

The realisation was first intimated through an unpublished thesis by Phillip Wren at Hull School of Architecture, where I had a part-time job around 1983. In this thesis, he pointed out that the growth of British shanties was a product of the urban population's successful struggle for increased leisure time. So, the shanties were specifically a product of proletarian struggle! Although there were clear influences at work, such as the use of colonial chalet-with-veranda kits, the architectural language also incorporated much that was unique. I realised that my attraction was based on a recognition of my own cultural heritage. I empathised with these slight structures more strongly than I did with a conventionally beautiful Palladian villa.

During the 1920s and 1930s the building of shanties was a serious generator of housing that could have challenged the mortgage ethos. However, shanties met with a virulent campaign of criticism, and one of the principal critics, as Phil Wren informed me, was Clough Williams-Ellis. He pronounced the shanties: 'England's most disfiguring disease'. He and his influential cronies led various campaigns against them, culminating in the 1947 Town & Country Planning Act, which brought all development under comprehensive municipal control. Ellis was also an author, and I was able to see a range of his published materials at the RIBA Library in Portland Place.

A year after Phil Wren had written his thesis, Dennis Hardy and Colin Ward published a comprehensive study of the whole phenomenon; *Arcadia for All, the Legacy of a Makeshift Landscape* (1984). I didn't see a copy of this until I ordered it from the publisher years later whilst doing this research.

The next chance event that influenced this line of thought was in 1989, when I came home in the middle of a TV programme, that was showing how William Morris's Arts & Crafts Movement had helped to create a romantic myth about the British countryside. This had contributed to the formation of a modern British national identity in preparation for the wholesale slaughter of the First World War. At the time, I didn't note the name of the programme or its director, as the implication of what I had seen sank in only slowly.

Later I found out from the erudite librarian Malcolm Taylor that the programme was called *'The Land of Lost Content'* and was produced by John Trifit based on research by Alun Howkins. The first half of the programme, which I had missed, had begun with the uncompromising statement: 'The countryside was always an impoverished place to live, paradise only for the privileged.' The great socialist hero William Morris, whose goodness was always held up as beyond reproach, had helped create a notion of Englishness which was based on a sanitised stereotype from a mythical golden age. This 'roses-round-the-porch' romantic interpretation of working-class heritage and the English landscape was presented as quintessentially English and jolly well worth dying for. This was one of the building blocks of the nationalism that swept up millions in the coming decades, leading inexorably to the unimaginable horrors of two world wars.

Could this really be the same William Morris, the immaculate socialist hero - the person every young artist with a social conscience was directed to revere. He was an enemy of imperialism, represented as sensitive to human suffering and to beauty and appreciative of the work of craftspeople - could this person really have contributed to the horrors of modern nationalism? Could this person have so misrepresented working-class history, driving people out of their communities to isolated suburban nightmares, fueled by false idealism? My suspicions mounted. Here was another gentleman-socialist who seemed to be involved in the crushing of proletarian cultural autonomy.

Later I bought a battered copy of the 1955 first edition of E.P. Thompson's *William Morris, Romantic to Revolutionary* from a secondhand book dealer. In spite of its 900 pages it was very readable, if you have a few weeks to spare. In spite of the author's somewhat adulatory attitude to Morris, it was still possible to spot many places in which his classism showed through. The later editions are shortened and leave some of these bits out.

Soon after this I went up to Luton, to see Graham Harwood's mural in a youth club, which resulted in the wordless 'IF Comic 1.' In the youth club's dustbin, I found a couple of copies of the *Folk Music Journal*. In one of these was a review of Dave Harker's book, *Fakesong; the Manufacture of British Folksong from 1700 to the Present Day*. This argues that Cecil Sharp, another well-bred gentleman socialist and a major figure in defining English folk music, had been busy misrepresenting working-class culture for the common good. Obviously, there was something going on here. Three in a row deserved further investigation - it seemed that the key to my own cultural alienation might be found here.

After several discussions with Howard Slater, who had been doing some parallel reading on the prehistory of the Labour Party, the picture was becoming clear. As the industrial revolution gathered strength, people were forced off the land and into towns. Between 1760 and 1860 seven million acres of commons were enclosed with a subsequent loss of commoners' rights. At the same time, primitive factory conditions demanded a workforce that could repeat mindless tasks in an endless daily routine. The destruction of traditional culture, with its cyclical sense of time, and native communalism, was required to achieve this proletarianisation. By 1860 more than half of the British population was living in towns and cities. In spite of the vicious exploitation and loss of traditions, the urban environment had its compensations.

As the cities developed people lived in greater concentrations than they had ever done before. Enormous numbers of people could be in contact with each other in the street; crowds could gather in response to events at short notice; clubs for self-education and intellectual debate had sprung up; the possibilities of mutual aid had grown, focused around the Pearly Kings and Queens, people had organised healthcare. The old paternal lord with his mansion on the hill became the more distant capitalist bosses. Although they controlled the factories with a rod of steel, their direct interference and cultural intimidation in everyday life was weak. Although drastically poor, working-class urban culture was dynamic, vibrant and autonomous. These radically new conditions caused human relations which were qualitatively different from anything that had gone before. The ruling class couldn't understand it. From their viewpoint, city street life seemed primitive, chaotic and full of fevered energy. Nonetheless they sensed the threat that it posed. What has been mythologised as a benign ‘community spirit' was the early growth of a potentially liberatory urban culture. If this rich culture had been allowed to mature and flourish, the class system could have become obsolete.

In his book, *Worship and Work*, published in Letchworth in 1913, Samuel Barnett, a leading philanthropist of the 1880s and one of the most prolific writers on the subject of culture and recreation in working-class life, “was convinced that the classes had become segregated in their pleasures, and that the poor were developing their own style of life which would eventually render them antagonistic to all established authority.” Waters, (1990) 68

The realisation of direct, unmediated political power depends on the ability of everyday culture to express, channel and evolve social needs.

The European revolutions of 1848 signaled the end of the European aristocratic monopoly of power. On the 10th April of the same year the Chartists, known for their quasi-autonomous cultural forms, petitions and monster rallies, gathered on Kennington Common in South London. The Chartists demonstrated the power of the new urban class. The threat of their march on Westminster had terrified the aristocracy and middle-classes and they had united to stop them by force of arms. From then on, the threat of the new urban class was taken seriously, with subsequent programmes of repression.

I originally typed this in a house built in the 1880s, reputedly for servants of Buckingham Palace. My house was then a crumbling squat in St Agnes Place, next to what was Kennington Common. After the Chartist meeting of 1848, the authorities acted quickly - the necessary legislation to enclose the common was put in motion and in 1850 the vicar of St Marks, the local church, promoted a scheme to make 'a place of resort for respectable persons'. The Prince Consort gave it his personal support and in March 1854 Kennington Park, with its formal layout, was created. I had been living there for nearly ten years before I became aware of this important historical site right on my own doorstep. It brought home to me the extent to which working-class history is repressed, and not just innocently lost in the mists of time.

I then met John Roberts, the art critic, who led me to the book by Chris Waters, *British Socialists and the Politics of Popular Culture 1884-1914* (1990). This book validated my mounting suspicions with a mass of historical material. At over £29, the book itself was beyond my pocket, so I obtained a free copy from the publisher by arranging to do a review for *Variant*, the radical arts magazine. According to Chris Waters, middle-class philanthropists, do-gooders and socialists had been at work since the 1850s to ensure that the new urban working-class were denied their own culture. Morris, Sharp and Ellis were just some of the more charismatic examples of many middle-class enthusiasts who led us well

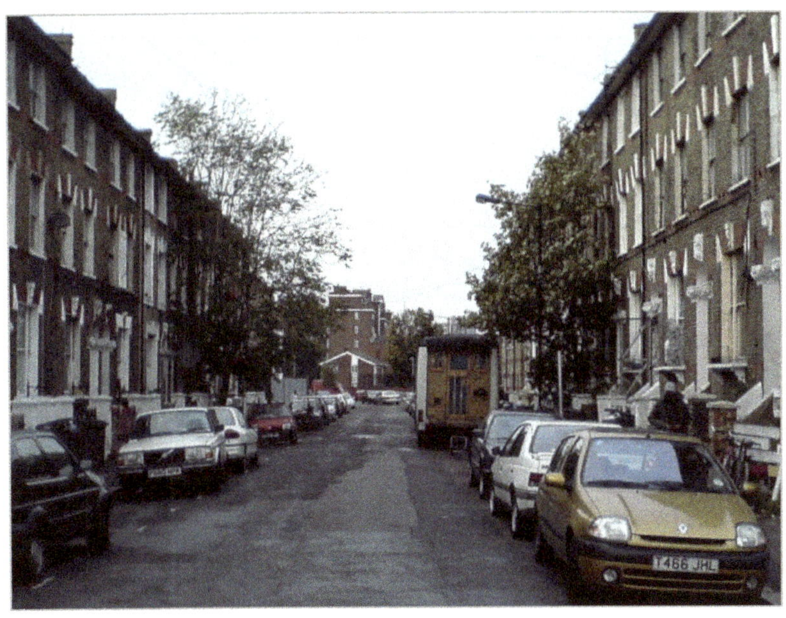

St Agnes Place, Kennington Park, 2005

and truly up the English country garden path.

This insight went a good way to explain the cultural paucity of my own suburban upbringing, the emptiness and disconnection I felt. If culture is something that grows organically out of desires and social conditions, then the culture of the lower-class suburbs, where I grew up, was either a cheap imitation of 'middle-class' manners or a shallow puddle of consumerism with all the perverse glamour and linear relation to needs that this implies. The deeper traditions had been erased from the clean Formica surface of our lives.

'Socialism' had been led, or taken over, by a series of well-heeled leaders who interpreted the 'elevation' of the working-classes almost entirely with their own values. Values that they arrogantly assumed were universal achievements and objective standards of excellence. These well-off socialists wanted to redistribute their civilised culture to all less fortunate members of humanity. For what people was not deserving of the benefits of civilisation? If they weren't grateful, it only proved they were racially deficient or irretrievably damaged by poverty. If they weren't able to recognise their good fortune, they were to be swept away. The people born to lead had a long and righteous tradition of the crusade to civilise the infidel and pagan. One God! One Civilisation! Onward Christian Soldiers!

In the middle of the most violent repression they convinced themselves of their generosity. After all, they were only doing people a good turn. Their vile victory was to persuade the majority of the people that their betterment only existed on bourgeois terms. At the same time, the people's incipient urban culture was damned as inferior, something to be ashamed of, to be hidden, to be discarded, to be denied, and where it persisted, to be destroyed.

The environmental mess left by the first flush of capitalism concerned the socially-aware philanthropists. They focused on reforms to improve sewerage, paving, industrial regulations and municipal government. Their concern was to tidy up and to make oppression hygienic and nice. To remove eyesores and leave only picturesque poverty. After the Chartists, the middle-class do-gooders realised they also needed to invest their time in actively civilising the lower orders.

From the 1860s, philanthropists tried to persuade the working-classes to spend their newly-won leisure time, with what came to be known as 'Rational Recreations'. This was activities like, choral singing, walks in the country, going to art galleries, reading books, promenading in the park and that sort of thing. We should spend our leisure on orderly pastimes in which little emotion is physically expressed or discussion likely. Although there is nothing wrong with any of these activities in themselves, we have to look at the whole package on offer: a package that represented the values which a person must adopt if they are to rise to better things, do well in life, become respectable and a good citizen. A person must give up working-class traits and to take up a banal and abridged version of middle-class demeanour and culture.

This is not to suggest that an ideal pure state of working-class culture ever existed. Chartism itself was a cultural movement as much as a political movement. It had its own associations which organised birth rites, funerals and other functions. It had their own songs, plays and literature, but middle-class taste was still an influence. 'Poetry had particular appeal for the Chartists, especially imitations of the verse of Shelley and Byron.' Wright (1988)140 quoting Kovalev (1971)57-73

The Chartist leaders William Lovett and John Collins wrote their '*New Move Manifesto*' in Warwick Jail and it was first published in 1840. In this they founded their hopes for the future on 'the right and influence of moral progress', which accepted the standards of middle-class taste as its model. 'Working-Class culture was something to be reformed through individual self-improvement'. Wright (1988)140

Later Socialist self-improvement schemes shared the same characteristics. They mainly succeeded in splitting those who became socialists from the majority of working people. Sensible refutation of alcohol became infused with classist separation. 'Self-imposed exclusion from the conviviality of the cup was often accompanied by forms of cultural elitism and the failure to reach those who held very different values.' Waters (1990)96

Ventures such as Leonards' Holiday camps, the Clarion Cycle Clubs and the Vocal Unions tended to cultivate exclusivity and reject those who failed to share their members' aspirations. Socialist clubs did not lead the working-class in any open way but created little islands in which those seeking a claim to a more respectable status could congregate.

The idea of 'respectability' is still powerful in class oppression. Generally emergent socialism was characterised by an alienation from working-class culture rather than arising from it. Socialist culture was 'narrow, corporate, defensive and marginal' shepherding people towards respectability and decorum in their cultural pursuits. The socialists attacked popular cultural forms like music hall, and when the picture palaces came in they laid into them as well. When the socialists later formed film clubs of their own, they were impregnated with middle-class values:

> The Film Society leaned more to the pompous than the proletarian e.g. An early programme note requested that, 'Members remind their guests that the society was founded for

> the purpose of technical study. Expression of emotion during the showing of the film may distract attention and therefore is to be avoided. Quoted in a review of *Deadly Parallels: Film and the Left in Britain 1929-39*, by Bert Hogenkamp (1986)

A couple of years before writing this book I accompanied a group of kids from the local adventure playground on one of their holiday trips to the local cinema to see *Karate Kid*. I was impressed by their response to the film. As the hero Karate Kid wins his glorious victory over the bullyboys the whole audience rose up with a wild and joyous scream of approval. This must have been the response of the early cinema-goers until the requirements of decorum got the better of them.

The working-class activities that couldn't be suppressed were commercialised. Although commericalisation encourages shallow diversions and less political content, it seemed to offer more scope for the expression of working-class desire and identity than that offered by the dry prescriptions and repressive moralism of 'rational recreations'.

Waters's book is a mine of information, but I was struck by one important shortcoming, which it shared with many other sources of information. The academic frame within which this valuable and hard-to-obtain knowledge exists requires a cool and 'objective' style. The result is that these books do not reflect or communicate the violent reality of class relations. Instead they reflect values of detachment. They do not register the outrage appropriate to the social injustices they are discussing. For a working-class reader, this engenders a strange aura of unreality.

On the other hand, it is difficult to seriously discuss history and produce knowledge from a working-class viewpoint outside of academia. Lack of time and money make access to source material and the atmosphere to discuss ideas difficult. An artist I knew had to steal the books he required to satisfy his intellectual appetite. If he had earned money to buy them there would be no time to read! In this introduction, I have tried to emphasize the often intuitive or chance means by which evidence has been found to show the difficulties of working outside the ivory towers. I also want to show how this text is embedded and motivated by my own life and by an outrage at class oppression. Both these things are disallowed or hidden in the academic text, but by presenting my argument in this way I risk forfeiting my place on the platform of serious discussion. (Which turned out to be largely true! Ed.)

The denial to people of their own culture is an act of violence, however 'nicely' it is done; however little bloodshed is apparent. It is an act of violence which, unless it is squarely faced, can reverberate through generations.

Reconstructing the story of working-class culture is a bit like making a jigsaw up from pieces found at jumble sales. The next piece turned up when an old friend from the Scratch Orchestra, Greg Bright, came to an exhibition I was having in an empty shop in London's Soho, organised by Alternative Arts. He brought a philosopher friend with him called Howard Caygill. Howard had written a book, *Art of Judgement*. Although it mainly focused on Kant on a level I wasn't qualified to follow, the first half of the book was taken up with a historical survey of the development of the philosophy of taste in Britain and Germany. These were two different traditions that Immanuel Kant had apparently tried to compare to transcend the 'bias of judgement'. The only problem, again, was that the book was unaffordable, so I had to wait for an interlibrary loan to get it. It was a difficult but exciting read, which seemed to validate my previous thinking as well as provide good information on the historical formation of British civil society and to show how central the idea of good taste was to its foundation and operation. Later this information was complemented by a remaindered copy of Victor J. Seidler's *Kant, Respect and Injustice*. This accessible book laid out the moral aspects of the Kantian legacy that validated some of my other ideas about oppression.

I was excited about all this material, and the fact that very few people have had the chance to see it assembled, much less in a readable form. As E.P. Thompson had pointed out, the serious study of working-class culture was only about twenty years old in 1990. Before this there was only 'folklore', which was derided as a mixture of curio collecting and 'crackpot fantasy'. I was determined to make a book out of my findings. I wrote a rough manuscript, which I passed around to Richard Hillman, Caroline O'Dwyer, Chris Saunders and Gabrielle Bown for comments. I'd like to thank them.

I also had a task to survey the surrounding literature to check that I was on course. This included wading through tomes like E.P. Thompson's *Cultures in Common* and Pierre Bourdieu's *Distinction*. This all took about a year and a half in whatever spare time I could find.

Finally, OK, there was no actual conspiracy of shadowy cloaked figures around a table; but the repression of working-class culture is so concerted that *it appears as if* there is a conspiracy. The thing that focused the projects of Morris, Sharp and Ellis was an ideology, a shared set of cultural values. Reading Bourdieu made me aware of just how intimately every object, action, gesture or expression that we use is ranked and policed by good taste. Much of our political resistance to oppression in the past has simply not taken account of the extent to which the status quo is maintained culturally.

Note on 2016 edition. The book has been edited for its reissue. At the time of first writing in 1993 I was not an academic. I have since got a PhD at London's Royal College of Art and worked at Westminster University. This experience has not made me change my opinion. I'm pleased to be able to reissue the book to a wider audience with some textual improvements and illustrations. The text has kindly been proofed by Julia Biggane.

Conspiracy of Good Taste

William Morris

Middle-class leaders of socialism and art.

> Morris's work as both as a designer and writer on the applied arts revolutionised the taste of the later nineteenth century, not only in Britain but in Europe and America. From a flyer for the William Morris Gallery, London (1993)

The artworld promotion of Morris holds him up as an icon of the truly socialist or humanitarian artist. In Britain, he is a household name familiar to almost any people with connections to 'the arts'. He represents ideals of connection to nature, unalienated craft work, utopian vision, civilised socialism and a kind of romantic stripped-pine aesthetic which still appeals to many. There is such an aura of respect around the myth that it is difficult to find critical studies amongst the many publications dealing with Morris and his part in the Arts & Crafts Movement. As the blurb above claims, his status extends throughout the western world and references to him are legion, most of them reverent. Undoubtedly, he was a person with many personal qualities, but even the most benign middle-class leaders were, and are, unwitting participants in class oppression.

> The rest of us are merely inventing methods of getting what we desire. William Morris taught us *what* to desire. Graham Wallas, quoted by Waters (1990)47

As mentioned in the introduction, culture was seen as a crucial site for indoctrination and the management of the 'impoverished' working-class personality. The 'intellectual heritage of the race', to which the working-class were invited to aspire, was of course the heritage of those upstairs.

On the Edge of Epping Forest

> I was born at Walthamstow in Essex in March 1834, a suburban

> village on the edge of Epping Forest, and once a pleasant place, but now terribly cocknified and chocked up by the jerry builder.
> William Morris in a letter to Andreas Scheu, 5.8.1883, quoted by Briggs (1962)29

Morris was born into an undistinguished and not particularly wealthy middle-class family. From the earliest age, he was imbued with romanticism and brought up with a love and knowledge of things medieval. Before the age of seven he was reading Walter Scott's novels and had been riding through the park on his Shetland pony dressed up in a miniature suit of armour. In 1840 the family moved to nearby Woodford Hall. This was rather grand, and run in a manner which had many 'medieval' aspects. The Hall brewed its own beer, churned its own butter and made its own bread. His father had his own coat of arms with a white horse's head. If the family did not have an ancient or noble lineage it certainly aspired to that style.

> In spite of his Welsh blood and of that vein of romantic melancholy in him, which it is customary to regard as of Celtic origin, his sympathies were throughout with the Teutonic stocks. Among all the mythologies of Europe the Irish myth... perhaps interested him least: for Welsh poetry he did not care deeply; and even the Arthurian legend never had the same hold on his mind, or meant as much to him, as the heroic cycle of the Teutonic race.
> Mackail (1899)13

Just before he went to Marlborough public school in 1847, his father died, leaving the family very wealthy. This wealth was from a lucky investment in mine holdings in Devon, which turned out to be extraordinarily rich in copper. We do not have much information on his early life and the influence of his parents. Frederick Kirchinoff attempts an analysis in *William Morris, the Construction of a Male Self, 1856-1872,* but with the slender evidence available, it is not too convincing. No doubt his father was a big influence.

> Morris remained, like his father before him, a business man. Years earlier, when he was simply living on his income, he had been unable to fix a coherent set of personal goals: it was not until he had grown used to the idea of running a business - that

he found a sense of direction. Kirchinoff (1990)19. See also Press & Harvey (1991)

At Marlborough, he read the medieval writers: Chaucer, Froissart, and particularly Malory's *'Morte d'Arthur'* and all things Arthurian. Being sent away to public school so soon after the death of his father must have been a huge emotional strain, if a similar experience of one close friend of mine is anything to go by. The public schools are an important arena for the conditioning of the oppressor class. This can be a cruel process in which there is rarely a place for compassion or grieving: 'Mr Fearon, the Secretary to the Charity Commissioners, who entered Marlborough in the same term, remembers him as fond of mooning and talking to himself, and considered a little mad by the other boys.' Mackail, p.17

Marlborough had only been established in 1843, and was rather disorganised by all accounts, so the boys had a degree of freedom which would be unheard of today. We know little of this period, but by his own account it was not a happy time. Morris is reported as having a wild temper and would resort to 'beating his own head, dealing himself vigorous blows, to take it out of himself.' Mackail (1899)43

Topsy Goes to Oxford

At the time Morris went up to Oxford University in 1853 there was talk of an alliance between the proletariat and the aristocracy under the leadership of Disraeli. This would clearly have appealed to Morris's medievalism and about this time he went through an aristocratic and 'high churchman' phase; then he was influenced by the Christian Socialists Charles Kingsley and F.D.Maurice.

His socialist and medieval interests met in Thomas Carlyle's *Past & Present* (1843). In this book, the life in a 12th century monastery was contrasted with a 'blistering old testament attack on the morality of industrial capitalism.' Morris continued to research medievalism and his studies of illuminated manuscripts and other artifacts embellished his earlier fantasies with endless authentic detail. For Morris, this romantic medieval dream world was increasingly becoming an alternative reality into which he could escape. Having this world with which he could compare contemporary conditions gave him some insights into current affairs, but the romance was strong and he was often carried away by it.

His main revelation at Oxford was undoubtedly the works of John Ruskin, whose chapter, 'The Nature of Gothic', from the second volume of *The Stones of Venice,* Morris later reprinted in a Kelmscott Press edition. Ruskin had many insights into the importance of pleasure and creativity in work. His writing was poetic and occasionally penetrating in its social analysis, in spite of the classist stereotypes.

> We have much studied, and much perfected, of late, the great civilised invention of the division of labour; only we give it a false name. It is not, truly speaking, the labour that is divided; but the men: -- Divided into mere segments of men -- broken into little fragments and crumbs of life; so that all the little piece of intelligence that is left in a man is not enough to make a pin, or a nail, but exhausts itself in making the point of a pin or the head of a nail. Ruskin (1852)

Ruskin's writing was internationally influential. He is considered the father of the Arts & Crafts Movement and was a constant influence on Morris throughout his life. Ruskin's interest in crafts and guilds was motivated by an authoritarian right-wing goal to establish a utopian feudalism.

At Oxford Morris met his lifelong friend Edward Burne-Jones. Together they formed a brotherhood whose aim was a 'crusade and holy warfare against the age'. This was a spiritual war and at one stage they even planned their own monastery.

The Poet

At Oxford Morris discovered he had a gift for writing poetry in the fashionable romantic style of the times exemplified by Robert Browning and Alfred Lord Tennyson. The romanticism of Percy Shelley had been a 'passionate protest against an intolerable social reality', inspired by 'Liberty, Equality, Fraternity'. With John Keats there is, Thompson claims, a proportion and tension maintained between escapism and harsh realities. Morris's first collection of poems was published in 1858. *The Defence of Guenevere,* had some of this tension, although the book sold less than three hundred copies and some of these were bought by Morris to give to friends. The Romantic movement believed in a utopia, the birth of which would be recast by its own poetry. This poetry had its own language, images, attitudes and conventions. Morris was imbued with these from early in his youth. He probably even thought in these terms, and when he came to put pen to paper he could be fluent in this idiom. By he wrote *Earthly Paradise* (1868), it was evident that his romanticism was little more than a yearning nostalgia, an escape from reality into youthful fantasy. However, this time it struck a chord with the times and was a huge success with the Victorian public!

> This endless poem, with its strong soap-opera element, was very popular for Victorian family readings and helped establish Morris in the public mind as a poet of arcadia, his images reinforcing the escapist mood. Marsh (1982)14

The future fame and glamour of Morris was largely founded on the popularity of this book. Most critics agree that his later romances are little but lightweight fantasy, a retreat to the safety of childhood memories. So, in short, the literature produced by this great socialist was slight. If you were a rebellious arty youth in the Sixties and probably since, you tended to be directed to William Morris. He was the man who was supposed to combine art and revolution. I can remember my own perplexed reaction on attempting to read Morris's poetry and romances as a young artist yearning for a way to end class oppression. I was puzzled that this sort of writing could be considered relevant to modern life. Cheap and maligned science fiction and detective novels had much more to say, and were written in a language I could relate to.

The Brotherhood

William Holman Hunt and John Everett Millais, two of the original Pre-Raphaelite Brotherhood (hereafter PRB), had apparently attended the Chartist meeting on Kennington Common on the 10th April 1848, but they were hardly Chartists. Their bohemian revolt was mainly against an increasingly suffocating middle-class respectability and hypocrisy. Morris and Burne-Jones had come to London in 1856 and been completely taken with Dante Gabrielle Rossetti at a time when the original PRB had broken up. Rosetti persuaded Morris to try his hand at painting. The two from Oxford gave new life to Rossetti's circle and it set off on a new round of bohemian revolt. Although this 'revolt' seems to have consisted of little more than hopping on and off furniture in enthusiastic discussion and other such ‘high jinks’.

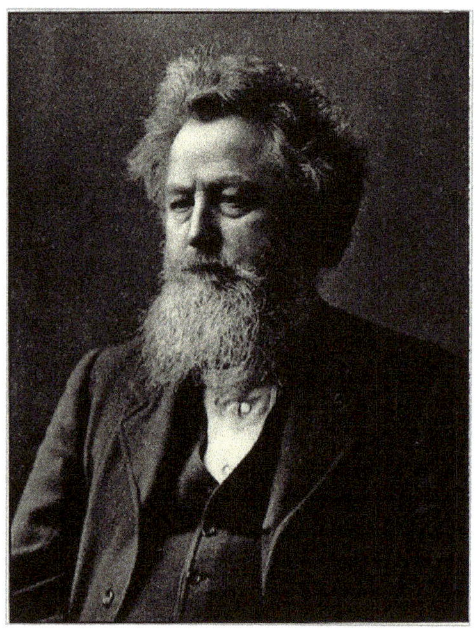

William Morris 1834 - 1896. Photograph by Eliot & Fry from the Internet Archive

Morris's wealth also allowed them to go to some lengths in drawing their medieval fantasies from life. Once the whole group went to Oxford to make a mural. Morris decided to have a complex piece of armour they required made by a local smith. Mackail reports:

> One afternoon when I was working high up on my picture, I heard a strange bellowing in the building, and turning round ... saw an unwonted sight. The basinet was being tried on, but the visor, for some reason would not lift, and I saw Morris embedded in iron, dancing with rage and roaring inside. The mail coat came in due time, and it was so satisfactory to its designer that the first day it came he chose to dine in it. It became him well; he looked very splendid. Mackail (1899)120

They seem to have achieved nothing but an impoverished sentimentalising of a lost age.

> Their exaggerated rejection of contemporary society ultimately led the Pre-Raphaelites into narcissism and futility. As an article in their own journal, *The Germ*, tried to point out, they missed 'the poetry of the things about us ... our railways, factories, mines, roaring cities, steam vessels and endless novelties and wonders produced everyday which if they were found only in the Thousand and One Nights or any poem classical or romantic, would be gloried over without end. Tames (1972)12

Art was Rossetti's religion and, as we would see it now, therapy. However, their dramatic disappointment in the world and retreat into fantasy can still, on occasion, exert a strong appeal, to judge from the recurrent enthusiasm for Pre-Raphaelite imagery.

They also attempted to live their fantasies. They constructed the ideal romantic woman and found living examples of the type, which Rossetti and Morris then married. The ideal was remote, unattainable and sad. They gave their melancholy and detachment from life the status of beauty.

> She was slim and thin... a little above the middle height of women, well-knit and with a certain massiveness about her figure... Her face, like her figure, had something strong and massive amidst its delicacy... dark brown abundant silky hair, a firm clear cut somewhat square jaw, and round well-developed lips... a straight nose with wide nostrils and perfectly made... high cheeks... and to light all this up, large grey eyes set wide apart. From an unpublished novel of 1870, quoted by Thompson (1955)93

Jane Burden's upward mobility

The 'ideal' woman he married, in April 1859, was Jane Burden, a working-class beauty Rossetti had discovered in Oxford.

Perhaps the young girl was swept into the role of Guenevere or

> Iseult before she herself had found out who she was ... It's hard to say whether she's a grand synthesis of all the Pre-Raphaelite pictures ever made - or they a keen analysis of her - whether she's an original or copy. Henry James, (1920)

Jane Burden's beauty was revered by the Pre-Raphaelite brotherhood and they idealised her body. She accepted her position on the pedestal but was 'unresponsive, silent, a poised, majestic presence ... The victim of unexplained ailments, which seem to have had some nervous origin.' Quoted by Thompson, (1955)197

She was perhaps just another sacrifice to modern glamour and the idealisation of love.

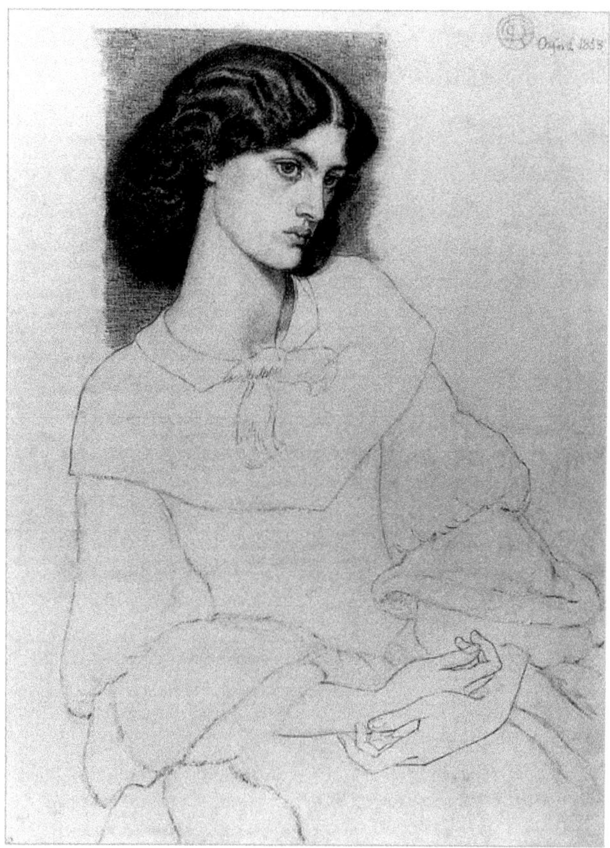

Jane Burden 1839 – 1914. drawing by D.G. Rosetti in 1858

> I fancy that her mystic beauty must sometimes have weighed rather heavily upon her ... She was a Ladye in a Bower, an ensorcelled Princess, a Blessed Damozel, while I feel she would have preferred to be a 'bright, chatty little woman' in request for small theatre parties and afternoons up the river. Graham Robertson, quoted by Thompson (1955)198

She was not only under pressure because of the idealisation of her body:

> It must be presumed that Jane was given a crash course in middle-class manners, etiquette and household management during the year between her engagement and marriage... Accent being the key index of class in Britain, she would learn how to speak 'properly' and be instructed in polite phraseology and expression. Marsh (1986)

These sentences are quoted from *Jane and May Morris: a biographical story 1839-1938* a book by Jan Marsh (1986) with no comment on the stress that such a forceful denigration of her upbringing would entail. This was not simply a change of culture, but one culture that defines itself by its disgust for the other, demanding its annihilation.

This was of course not an isolated case. In about 1860 the massively influential *Mrs Beeton's Book of Cookery and Household Management* appeared for the first time. Much of what Jane had to learn was detailed in Mrs Beeton's famous tome. (There was a copy around when I was young which goes to show what a ubiquitous bible of manners it became. I remember thinking that it was referred to with awe just because it was so thick.) The upward mobility process was violent enough to cut her off from her family:

> There is no evidence that she did seek out any family connections ... Her mother had died in Oxford earlier in the year, on 2nd Feb 1871, at the age of 66. Jane did not go to the funeral... Neither of her daughters seems to have recalled meeting their Burden grandmother... If they were not taken to see their granny, it must have been because the social gulf was considered unbridgeable. Marsh (1986)

There is no record of how she felt after the death of her father, aged 55, in 1865. Afterwards her sister Bessie came to stay but 'nothing is recorded of Bessie's personality ... Morris complained of her being dull.' How different would have been the attention she got if she had been a beauty like Jane. Throughout Jan Marsh's book one is struck by the lack of any outrage or feeling on these issues. In her other general study of the Pre-Raphaelite women she does at least comment:

> The enclosed rooms in which these ladies live, looking out on inviting sunlit landscapes, and the tangled strands binding their vigorous limbs, are surely metaphors of women's conditions, signifying the docile, passive, reflective and domestic role that dominated Victorian ideas of femininity. Marsh (1987)

Morris had fallen for an idealised image, one transfixed by the pain of her displacement. He never seemed connected with her as a close friend and his marriage was not a happy one. It was with this background of an unhappy marriage that Morris came to Revolutionary Socialism. However, Socialism never helped him analyse the class problems of this relationship, never mind solve it. Yet it seems that such issues may be at the heart of alienation.

It was not always a case of rich upper-class men choosing beautiful or sexy working-class women. The reverse may be illustrated in the famous partnership of Beatrice and Sidney Webb, perhaps the most influential individuals in the moulding of British socialism. Although the middle-class Beatrice was sorry for the lower classes and admired the qualities they retained in the extreme adversity that they endured -

> She 'showed a particularly haughty and contemptuous attitude towards the lower middle-class and she was never surprised when she found members of it lacking in self-control or in true refinement of manners. Royden Harrison quoted in Levy (1987)53

If they did not conform properly to good taste and give up working-class mannerisms and culture they were to be derided. It was the working classes who went up in the world, and wanted to take their culture with them, who were the real threat. Sidney had a lower-class upbringing on the edge of poverty and had risen through the Civil Service by a consistent chain of examination successes. Accordingly: 'She was merciless in her dealings with him. He had to stop wearing grubby shirts, stop dropping his aitches, stop talking about what he would do when he was prime minister. He had also to stop writing to her in terms which suggested anything remotely of lust.' Royden Harrison in Levy (1987)54

The subjugation of Sidney Webb to the middle-class ideals took a heavy toll on him. When asked later why he would not write his autobiography he answered that he could not because he had 'no inside'. The working-class soul is a social entity - by giving up your identity you give up your connection to that soul.

The Firm and The Art & Crafts Movement

After his spell of painting with Rossetti, Morris's next project with his architect friend Phillip Webb, was to build The Red House at Bexleyheath in 1859. It was described by a visitor as 'vividly picturesque'. The brotherhood were invited to design the fixtures and fittings and the success of this venture led to the formation of The Firm.

The Firm, managed and run by Morris, became his way of waging 'holy warfare against the age'; but the age was undeterred - the Firm's work was mainly confined to the luxury market. By the mid 1880's the Arts & Crafts were already being considered by many of his clients and admirers as a sufficient end in itself. W.R. Letharby observed: 'The national arts had been flattened out and destroyed in the name of gentility, learning and taste.' Quoted by Thompson (1955)128

Outside of The Firm, the Arts & Crafts Movement in reality produced very little of note. The Clarion Handicraft Guild was one of the larger organisations inspired by Morris. By 1904 it had 30 branches throughout Britain and was holding annual exhibitions of its work. The exhibition in 1902 did not impress Montague Blatchford, the eminent socialist, who commented that the work displayed was 'amateurish, imitative and not particularly useful'. In 1907 the strength of the Guild began to wane and the exhibition of that year was even called *rubbish* by A.J. Penty, an otherwise enthusiastic supporter of Arts & Crafts. The movement had lost any remnants of a political critique.

The Arts & Crafts Movement did not occur in isolation. Following similar themes were painters of picturesque landscapes, novelists and garden designers like Gertrude Jeykyll.

> In the innocent enthusiasm of the books she wrote, Gertrude Jekyll helped forge these fantasia, however much she wanted to dispel them. Her nostalgia for 'olde countrye' life hid forever the poverty behind the painting. Trifit (1989)

Jekyll was a brilliant gardener who, as the middle-class fashion for a country retreat took off, advocated a contrived naturalism making an 'authentic' English country garden. The illustrations in her popular books, reprinted many times, are usually of very grand old country mansions. She also bought old rural cottage furniture and helped create a rural antiques demand. Soon enough the labourers' houses were furnished with cheap mass-produced veneered pieces in place of the sturdy old stuff bought by the middle-class dealers. This old rural simply crafted and sturdy furniture provided the model for the Arts & Craft aesthetic.

In the context of an already well-developed romantic interpretation of the southern English landscape the mythical ideals produced by the ruralist movement were powerful. The Arts & Crafts Movement of Ruskin and Morris, along with the efforts of Sharp, Williams-Ellis and many others, formed an Arcadian ethos that became a cornerstone of modern nationalism. The old rural artefacts and 'folk' customs were repackaged as 'emblems of patriotism'. The First World War, a war of unprecedented scale, ferocity and horror, was fought from these ideas of national identity. More than one working-class writer has cynically interpreted the way this war was fought as simply an exercise in culling the working-class:

> The old men of the upper classes who were in command possessed the half-concealed knowledge that if they did not dispose of them in this roulette-wheel fashion then those millions would turn round and sweep them away. Sillitoe (1972)114

More tragically the carnage simply encouraged further need for escapism and the arcadian myth was transfixed in the pain and loss of all those brothers, husbands and sons sacrificed for their country.

> The very labourer, with his thatched cottage and narrow slip of ground, attends to their embellishment. The trim hedge, the grass-plot before the door, the little flowerbed bordered with snug box, the woodbine trained up against the wall, and hanging its blossoms about the lattice, the plot of flowers in the window, the holly, providentially planted about the house, to cheat winter of its dreariness, and to throw in a semblance of green summer to cheer the fireside: all these bespeak the influence of taste, flowing down from high sources, and pervading the lowest levels of the public mind. Washington Irving, quoted by Jones (1912)

This suggests that the conscious humanitarian motives and strategies Morris undoubtedly had were overwhelmed by the unconscious class values in which they were embedded. His later 'international' socialism did not annul the damage of the Arts & Crafts Movement. Because socialism didn't challenge the basis of taste, it was the vehicle for it. Morris continued to adhere to Ruskin's ideas of art and architecture throughout his conversion to Marxist socialism. We might even presume to let Ruskin speak for the underlying values Morris held:

> Of course I am a Socialist - of the most stern sort - but I am also a Tory of the sternest sort. Ruskin, 1886, in a letter to Cockerell, quoted by Swenarton (1989)169

Morris was not 'of the sternest sort' but his values were still those of the rentier class in spite of his professed ideals. Along with Ruskin, Morris held essentially perverse upper-class notions of work, notions that romanticised and raised manual labour above all other work and especially above the reproductive work of women. If work didn't result in objects it is simply not real work. The fetishisation of the male body as warrior, harking back to the Teutonic Cycle, is transferred to the heroic manual worker, an image that found its home in both Stalinist and Nazi iconography.

Architecture was central to Morris's ideas and yet even with all the talk of manual labour there was no real relationship to the building site. The medieval Guilds of Freemen, which were such a model for

Ruskin and Morris, soon became used by people such as A.J. Penty as a method of curtailing class struggle in the building industry. Penty was an overtly fascist supporter of 'Guild Socialism'. This movement collapsed in the winter of 1922-23. (See Swenarton (1989)169)

The myths about work and the nature of the landscape, forged in the nineteenth century are still going strong today. They are institutionalised in our heritage and conservation industries, and in the minds of all those who aspire to respectability and good taste. An example is The National Trust. If it is true that half of us visit the countryside twelve times a year or more, 'Eager to preserve a pastoral ideal and create the landscape of his imagination, urban man is neglecting social and agricultural realities.' Hewison (1993)

Morris started the Kelmscott Press after the Socialist League failed in 1890. His intention, according to his early biographer and friend Aymer Vallance, was to produce a 'perfect and lasting monument before he should die and pass away'. Morris believed that the 'only work of art that surpasses a complete medieval book is a complete medieval building'. One of his earliest editions published in 1892 was Ruskin's *The Nature of Gothic*. We should note that he never considered publishing the work of his working-class comrades who had given so much to the struggle.

Much was made of the intricate attention paid to every stage of design and production of Kelmscott editions. The paper was 'hand-made from the linen shirts of certain peasants.' Vallance (1897). All said and done, this was nothing but an escape.

> William Morris's romantic late Nineteenth century century attempt to infuse the printing trades with higher values now seems like a misguided sentiment buoyed up by a sea of money.
> Betsy Davids and Jim Petrillo, 'The Artist as Book Printer' in Lyons (1985)

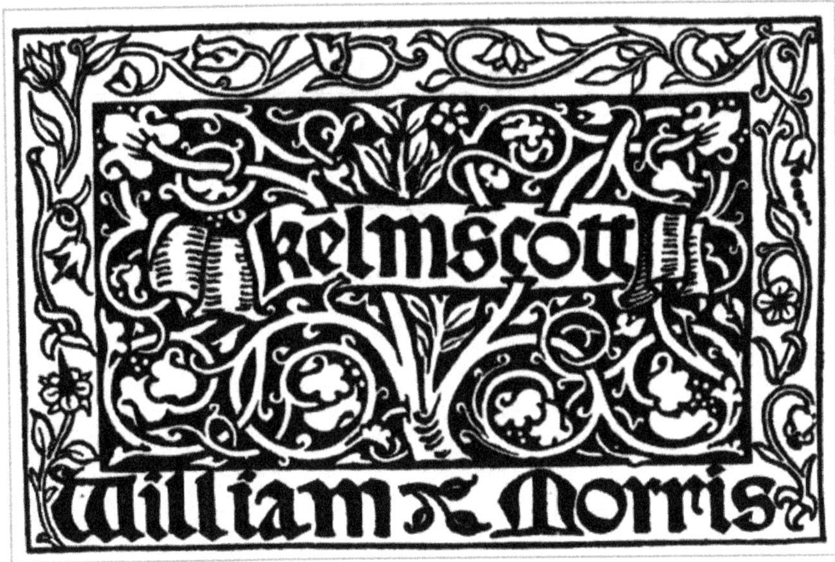

Socialists Rich...

It was wealthy men who led and financed the groups which had their own papers and which made the running in the official history of British Socialism. H.M. Hyndman, the 'father of British Socialism', had a terrific air of confidence about him. A wealthy middle-class man, just over forty, typical perhaps of the class of empire builders, he organised a union of the autonomous London radical clubs that led to the formation of the Social Democratic Federation (SDF) in 1881. Hyndman, something of a jingoist on the quiet, became leader of this SDF and financed the paper *Justice*. Morris joined the SDF in January 1883, but later split, on the issue of parliamentary strategies, and formed the Socialist League with its paper *Commonweal*. The League and its paper were financed by Morris to the tune of £500 a year, which was a small fortune at the time.

Morris also managed and sponsored his own Hammersmith branch of The League and provided the premises. The measure of their dependency was that when Morris died the branch fell apart. The same was true earlier of *Commonweal*. It folded soon after Morris withdrew his support. Historians tend to play down or ignore how wealth creates artificial organisations and distorts individual contributions. Consider the different tone E.P. Thompson uses in the following two extracts:

> Morris had already made a serious sacrifice to the Cause, raising money from the sale of some of the most treasured early books in his private collection ... Tom Mann selling all his personal possessions down to his kitchen table in order to keep the propaganda alive in Newcastle. Thompson (1955)371 & 563

Notice how Thompson only uses the word 'sacrifice' when he writes about Morris's sale; but who actually made the greater sacrifice? The wealthy socialists, including Morris and Engels, would also fund a few selected agitators with 'workhouse rations'. This sort of patronage would have exerted a powerful directing influence on the movement. Not to say that it was not resisted. At one time Engels required J.L Mahon to submit to his son-in-law Edward Aveling's direction if he wished to receive funds. As the upper class Aveling was a profligate, a fact which was widely known, though possibly not to Engels, Mahon refused. Later Mahon's stand was vindicated in the saddest of circumstances when Eleanor Marx was driven to suicide as a result of Averling's behaviour.

Socialists Poor - Tom Maguire

I want to spend some time describing the life of the best working-class agitator in The League. My aim is first, to offset the tendency to dwell on the study of upper-class heroes whilst their working-class counterparts go unmentioned; working-class people do not own the publishing houses or academies necessary to research and publish their own histories. Secondly, I aim to contrast the work of Morris with a working-class artist who was really connected to the people.

In 1883, a seventeen-year-old Catholic working-class photographer picked up a copy of *The Christian Socialist* from the Secular Hall bookstall in Leeds. He was immediately hooked and began looking for other people to put its ideas into action. By hanging around Vicar's Croft, the popular 'spouting place', he had soon gathered a small group who formed a branch of the SDF.

> Early in 1885... Strolling through the Market place of Leeds, my attention was attracted by a pale but pleasant featured young fellow, who in a clear voice was speaking to a motley crowd. After listening for a while I began to feel a strong sympathy with his

> remarks, and what is more - a sudden interest in and liking for the speaker; and I remember how impatiently I waited for his reappearance on the following Sunday. Alf Mattison in Ford (1895)

Within a year of the League's split from the SDF, at the end of 1884, Tom Maguire was criticising Morris's *Commonweal* paper for being boring and written in a language unsuitable for the workers. Morris was stung by the criticism but decided that the 'literary character of the paper should be maintained.' In spite of this snub, Maguire followed up his criticism in his usual practical way with an article titled: 'The Yorkshire Miners and their Masters'. This was the first detailed article on the conditions of workers carried in the *Commonweal.*

Maguire was ambitious as a writer and planned a clear textbook of socialist theory in accessible language. 'People call themselves socialists,' he wrote, 'but what they really are is just ordinary men with socialist opinions hung around, they haven't got it inside of them.' Ford (1895). His *Machine-Room Chants,* inspired by his organising work with the tailoresses and occasional verse in socialist papers, stand out from other socialist versifying of the time by reason of their greater range and realism. 'Socialists looked more to middle-class writers for their material than to workers.' Waters (1990)120. Most of the poets in the Commonweal were 'pallid, overstrained and romantic', dealing only in clichéd symbols and archetypes.

> Maguire wrote directly from his own experience: he was a forerunner of the poetry of Tressell, he did not romanticise the working people, but described them with all their weaknesses, without condescension and with an underlying faith in their power. In his versatility, his cultural achievements, his enthusiasm and self-sacrifice, he typified all that was best in the Socialist League. And he was perhaps the most able working-class agitator the League produced. Thompson (1955)619

In spite of the above eulogy, Thompson refers to Maguire as a 'mouthpiece of Morris' when all the evidence points to his originality and independence of thought. Just because he stayed in the League until the end does not imply a servile loyalty.

In 1889, the year of The Great Dock Strike, there was a great surge of confidence amongst the unskilled workers. This kept Maguire and his friends busy helping various new unions that were forming. This activity was in contrast to the passivity of the League in London, although branches in Manchester, Aberdeen and Bradford were also active. Unfortunately, this intense period of activity also led to the group splitting on the question of the use of violence.

Maguire and Alf Mattison then joined the Fabian Society. At the time, there was a general attempt to infiltrate the Fabians, which provoked some alarm amongst its middle-class leadership, but in the end the radical provincial groups, who these people represented, joined the Independent Labour Party (ILP) and the Fabians breathed a sigh of relief. Maguire had great hopes for the ILP but was soon disillusioned. The intrigues of the ILP depressed him.

> I want to get away from your damn party politics and silly quarrels ... We get mixed up in disputes among ourselves ... and can't keep a straight line for the great thing. Maguire quoted by Ford (1895)

In the winter of 1893 he was running *The Labour Champion*, a militant trade unionism paper, in Leeds and engaged in agitation on the question of unemployment, the pain of which he was to know only too well from his own situation in the bitter and desperate winters of 1894-95. Profoundly moved by the suffering caused by unemployment at this time before social benefits, he wrote a passionate 'Out o' Work's Prayer':

> O God of Humanity, gaze on me, powerless, pulseless, and spent,
> Shrunken of muscle and withered of heart and of mind,
> With all that was hope in me strangled, distorted, broken and bent,
> All that was man in me loosened and left far behind...

On February 10th 1895, he was lecturing on the theme of 'Labour Federation'. Three weeks later Alf Mattison heard that he was ill, and hurrying to his home, where he lived with his mother, found him suffering from pneumonia, without food or fire in the house. The aid of comrades came too late, and two days later, on March 8th, Tom Maguire died... The people lined the streets for two miles when the funeral procession, 1000 strong, went by. No other man in Yorkshire had given such long and such notable service to the cause; and yet, this man at his death, was only twenty-nine. Thompson (1955)705

But the last word should go to Maguire:

> Political progress is not made after the fashion of a Corydon-Phyllis dance, jigging along ... through pleasant places with the sun shining over us. Ford (1895)

...and Socialists Famous

It was not only the wealth of the upper-class socialists that influenced the movement. People such as Prince Kropotkin had a tremendous glamour, which had an effect on the young working-class radicals. Engels comments incisively on what a powerful allure this could be in a letter to H. Schluter in 1890:

> The most repulsive thing here is the bourgeois 'respectability' which has grown deep into the bones of the workers ... I am not at all sure for instance, that John Burns is not secretly prouder of his popularity with Cardinal Manning, the Lord Mayor and the bourgeoisie in general than of his popularity with his class. And Champion ... has intrigued for years with bourgeois and especially conservative elements ... Even Tom Mann, whom I regard as the finest of them, is fond of mentioning that he will be lunching with the Lord Mayor. If one compares this with the French, one can see what a revolution is good for after all. Thompson (1955)668

> Some of the pioneers (if Bruce Glasier's recollections can be trusted) regarded Morris with an awe, which was near to being sickly. To them he seemed a figure of romance, coming from the glamorous and fairy tale world of the Pre-Raphaelite Romantics. G.B. Shaw, quoted by Thompson (1955)351

Of course, not everyone was taken in by the glamour, although those that opposed it, like Dan Chatterton, tended to be 'mad' outsiders. Archivists and historians do not tend to record such incidents when the heroes are challenged, and when they do, rarely treat them as significant.

> Max Nettlau, who witnessed Chatterton haranguing William Morris at the Autonomie Club in January 1890, recorded with sadness: 'the most beautiful words of Morris woke in the old man nothing but the remark that hanging was nevertheless necessary for the public good.' quoted by Whitehead (1984)

Hyndman always wore his top hat and frockcoat to rallies and was fond of mocking his audience by thanking them for 'supporting his class'. Morris and Hyndman were both noted for their imposing presence, writing fluency and influential contacts. Morris's Hammersmith clubroom was a fashionable meeting place for the young avant-garde; H.G. Wells was amongst them in his red tie; so was W.B. Yeats. Morris had a mythic reputation as the picturesque author of *The Earthly Paradise* and manager of The Firm with its salubrious premises in Oxford Street. It seems that the working-class members had to put up with snobbery from such fellows - but were also mesmerised by their glamour.

The Great Class Gulf

> On Sunday, I went a-preaching Stepney way. My visit intensely depresses me as these Eastwards visits always do; the mere stretch of houses, the vast mass of utter shabbiness and uneventfulness, sits upon one like a nightmare; of course, what slums there are one doesn't see. You would perhaps have smiled at my congregation; some twenty people in a little room, as dirty as convenient and stinking a good deal. It took the fire out of my fine periods, I can tell you: it is a great drawback that I can't talk to them roughly and unaffectedly. Also, I would like to know what amount of real feeling underlies their bombastic revolutionary talk when they get to that. I don't seem to have got at them yet - you see this great class gulf lies between us all. Quoted from a letter to Mrs Burne-Jones 1885, Meier (1978)40 and Tames (1972)36

The problem for these leaders of men, who felt that they were pioneers in a new social order, was that they knew little about the people that they were meant to be leading. What knowledge they had was coloured by their class viewpoint. Hyndman thought that they were 'never quite conscious agents of history themselves' whilst to Morris they were 'good fellows enough, who had only to be got to listen to reason.' The nature of class oppression and the differences that created this gulf were not understood. Although there were upper-class people like Henrietta and Samuel Barnett, who were obsessed with the question of communication between the classes, nobody could think clearly in this area. This is not surprising, as the key way the oppressor class is prepared for its role is to develop a mental blank in their perception of the oppressed, and a way that the working-class is prepared for its role is to 'learn' that what they have to say is of little or no importance.

The culture of the capitalist class was, above all, one of books. Morris believed that the subject of socialism was 'a difficult and intricate one, and to understand it really requires a great deal of reading.' Morris letter to R. Thompson, 24th July 1884, quoted by Swenarton (1989)80. The notion that working-class liberation depends on reading books seems particularly ludicrous to me, and I'm sure it would have done to working-class people of the time.

This gulf between the classes was also evident in their publications. When Morris wrote the manifesto of the League it was his instructions to them rather than something that was based on their demands. Generally, the publications from the League suffered from a detachment from the lives of the majority of the population. When their theory didn't communicate, it was thought to be because it was too detailed or too complicated for simple minds. Really, it was detail that was missing! The point was that it was too abstract and rarely came down to earth. Broad historical generalisations that did not connect with a lived reality were not so much incomprehensible as boring. They never included anecdotes and facts from the lives of the readership.

The implication was that a lack of intelligence or at least education was the problem. The truth was, Morris's words did not connect to the lived experience of workers nor to their language:

> I gave my 'Monopoly' (lecture) at the Borough of Hackney Club, which was one of the first workman's clubs founded, if not the first; it is a big club, numbering 1600 members; a dirty wretched

place enough, giving a sad idea of the artisans' standard of comfort: the meeting was a full one, and I suppose I must say attentive, but the comings and goings all the time, the pie boy and the pot boy, was rather trying to my nerves: the audience was civil and inclined to agree, but I couldn't flatter myself that they mostly understood me, simple as the lecture was. William Morris's Diary, 27 March 1887

The Commonweal paper had similar problems. We have already heard how the literary 'standard' of *The Commonweal* was the barrier over which working-class contributors were required to leap. There was apparently no agitational policy at all. Only in one pamphlet by Edward Averling, *'The Factory Hell,'* do we see any attempt at an analysis of working conditions.

What should have been one of Morris's most useful publications, *Socialism, its Growth and Outcome,* co-written with Ernest Belfort Bax, was spoilt by its lack of examples which related to working-class life. Apart from this, the book also included moral diatribes and condescending attitudes. The generalised image of working-class people, in the mind of the middle-class socialists was based not on scientific study or direct contact with working-class life. All that was left was a cloud of classist myths and stereotypes of working people. In spite of this Thompson, almost comically, repeatedly insists that Morris's socialism was scientific. However, 'correct' his Marxist analysis was, it was hard for him to get away from the 'moral improvement' of the working-class.

Working-Class Anger

An unfriendly observer of the Hammersmith Branch of the League gives us some insight into its composition. 'It needed but a glance over this assembly to understand how very theoretical were the convictions that had brought its members together.' Quoted by Thompson (1955)498. Morris attracted the middle class interested in a 'pure' socialism, whilst the East End branches of the League tended to be working class and attracted to anarchistic communism. Maybe Anarchy best expressed the class hatred and the outrage at the blatant injustice of class oppression, and a belief in people's ability to take power into their own hands.

This anger was something even Morris, with his recurrent temper, could never hope to understand. A good illustration is to be found in Dan Chatterton's response to Lord Brabazon, guest speaker at the Clerkenwell branch of the SDF in 1887:

> Chatterton who, for all his diatribes against the aristocracy had never got a chance of giving one of its members 'a bit of his mind', was naturally on hand. The noble philanthropist had just been round the world and was full of emigration as a panacea for the congested poverty of the old country. He discoursed on the subject for an hour, to the amusement of the audience of which no member could have raised the price of a railway ticket to Clacton-on-Sea, much less the fare to Canada.
>
> Then Chatterton struggled on to the platform and poured out his indignation. Gaunt, ragged, unshaven, almost blind he stood, the embodiment of helpless furious poverty, and shaking his palsied fist in Brabazon's face, denounced him and his efforts to plaster over social sores, winding up with a lurid imaginative account of the Uprising of the People and a procession in which the prominent feature would be the head of the noble lecturer on a pike. I shall never forget Lady Brabazon's face while this harangue was delivered. H.H. Champion, quoted by Whitehead (1984)

There is an important difference between an expression of anger using images of violence, and its actual realisation or a proposal for its realisation. A liberation struggle needs to differentiate quite clearly between the inevitable, and sometimes useful, expression of angry fantasy and irrational policies of violence. Here lies the border between sanity and madness.

Good Taste censors the expression of such outrage or dismisses it as having no part in the production of legitimate knowledge. Yet an outraged rant, replete with violent imagery, may be all that can fully communicate the experience of injustice, quite apart from the cathartic effect it may have on the ranter.

Working-Class 'Ignorance'

> The frightful ignorance and want of impressibility of the average English workman floors me at times. William Morris's Diary, 1887, quoted by Thompson, 1955, p.507

Morris describes his audience at a typical radical club:

> The sum of it all is that the men at present listen respectfully to Socialism, but are perfectly supine (earlier; taken with no enthusiasm, puzzled.) and not inclined to move except along the lines of radicalism and trades unionism ... the working men listened attentively trying to understand, but mostly failing to do so ... I doubt if most of them understood anything I said; though some few of them showed they did by applauding the points. ... I felt very down cast amongst these poor people in their poor hutch. ... A fresh opportunity (if I needed it) of gauging the depths of ignorance and consequent incapacity of following an argument which possesses the uneducated averagely stupid person. Diary, quoted by Thompson, 1955, p.508-10

Thompson then comments with wonderful understatement and bemusement: 'To some degree he did not understand the people he most wanted to reach.' What is coming over in these quotes is a terrible reinforcement of the central tenet of working-class oppression, the supposed lack of intellectual capability.

> The dominant language discredits and destroys the spontaneous political discourse of the dominated. It leaves them only silence or a borrowed language, whose logic departs from that of popular usage but without becoming that of erudite usage, a deranged language, in which the 'fine words' are only there to mark the dignity of the expressive intention, and which, unable to express anything true, real or 'felt', dispossesses the speaker of the very experience it is supposed to express. Bourdieu (1984)462

It is easy to misunderstand the distraction caused by the bind of daily oppression, and its echoes from our early life, as a lack of intelligence. This distraction may often be dispelled by simply bringing people's attention away from their misery and on to the matter presently at hand. This might be achieved by respectfully acknowledging their presence by asking for names, and other basic questions that denote some respect for each individual. That still leaves the question of language and terminology. A problem with communication is often interpreted by those in the dominant position as a lack of intelligence.

It was only in April 1887 that Morris, addressing striking Northumberland miners, got a realistic picture of the power and intelligence of working-class people for the first time. He had not really listened to working-class people and thought that stupefying poverty had addled their brains. What he did not realise was that his grand presence itself would have intimidated many working-class people and prevented them from showing their true intelligence, which even then might take a form not immediately recognised by a middle-class witness. If I am right that class oppression does temporarily interfere with the functioning of our intelligence, it is also true that an uprising can quickly clarify the mind.

It was only the work of agitators in The League in the north of England, quite distant from Morris, like Mahon and Maguire, that was effective in forming active workers' movements. In reports of their speeches we see that they are presenting things in straightforward, practical terms - not at all the same thing as ‘simple'.

The transformation of the image of the working-class that occurred during the Dock Strike of 1889 is instructive. The 'criminal classes' of bourgeois fiction proved their power and ability for disciplined revolt and were to be seen marching through London, self-organised in disciplined ranks. In spite of this The League and the SDF held a lofty detachment to what was happening in the streets. The same is true of Fabian socialists like Beatrice Webb.

> The dockers whom she had sadly written-off as incorrigible sensualists, incapable of self-discipline and virtually devoid of hope or ambition organised themselves into a trade union and staged one of the most triumphant strikes in the history of British labour. Royden Harrison, in Levy (1987)54

The Great Lancashire Cotton Strike of 1884 was the only time that The League made serious contact with industrial workers en masse when Morris and Hyndman went up to address a mass meeting, but the class gulf and the upper-class attitudes of the speakers made leadership difficult.

> The difficulty he had adapting himself to working-class audiences. Despite his burning sympathy and zeal of his new conversion; he could not rid himself of a superior attitude. Meier (1978)40

> I may say without fear of contradiction that we of the English middle-classes are the most powerful body of men the world has yet seen, and that anything we have set our heart upon we will have. Morris quoted by Meier (1978)35

William Morris's Good Taste

Morris's aesthetic remained close to the ideas expressed by Ruskin in *The Nature of Gothic* and are not only irredeemably romantic but also quite rigid. Even our Morris fan Edward Thompson admits that Morris does not recognise the 'active agency' of art. (see Thompson, 1955, p.763).

His art had to be heroic or sweet, epic or soothing - a solace. The subtitle of his famous utopia, *News from Nowhere,* is '*An Epoch of Rest*'. He hated the Social Realists and the Impressionists; even Shakespeare was dubious. His only advice to people who wanted beauty was to 'Look back! Look back!' Art should be for repose and escape. He wanted the artist to have the sympathy of 'simple people'; but these people existed only in myth.

E.P. Thompson claims that Morris' writings on art are amongst his greatest achievements, but at the same time he admits that he failed to have a consistent theory. In keeping with his time, his idea of culture was rigidly elitist and he could only connect his taste in art with his 'scientific' socialism in the most idealistic ways. His love of romantic verse only spoke to the comrades because they had already grown accustomed to romantic verse being thrust on them as an uncontestable form of excellence.

> The city is 'wicked' and a 'hell', like Shelley's 'London': the lives of the workers are 'squalid' and 'sordid', and they are 'poor ghosts' who 'droop and die'. The sense of 'crowds' as something oppressive is present. Morris rarely expresses any sense of vitality in the working-class, but only the Cause itself, the hope of the future. Thompson (1955)775

This fear of 'the masses' is taken up later by many intellectuals and writers, such as H.G. Wells. See Carey (1992).

If Morris's poetry was stifled with all the words, images and rhythms of Romanticism then his later romances were worse. The Fabian George Bernard Shaw saw them as 'a startling relapse into literary Pre-Raphaelitism'.

The importance of poetry amongst the working-class intelligensia was much more significant than it is today. In the intellectual and lively atmosphere of metropolitan clubland of the 1870s, poetry had a place which is difficult for us to imagine today. Poetry still had a connection with the oral; with the sounds of words. Not that many worker poets got published, but it is perhaps not surprising if we assume Morris's attitudes were widely shared in the Literary world. In his pamphlet *Club Life and Socialism in Mid-Victorian London* (1983), Stan Shipley mentions J.B Leno, a Chartist who in 1864 was also on the First International (The General Council of The International Working Man's Association) as a notable exception.

Morris's letters to an aspiring young worker poet in response to his request for criticism of his poetry give us an insight into how formal, narrow and exclusive were the rules that defined 'good' poetry. The poet in question, Fred Henderson, was a socialist pioneer in Bradford and then Norwich.

> Horace was right in saying that neither gods nor men can stand mediocrity in a poet: it is like colour in art, it must be either right or wrong, it cannot be 'pretty good'. Thompson (1955)875

By now we know from comparative anthropology that the meanings of colours are culture-specific (red as warm, blue as cold, may be the only universal); but Morris saw middle-class language and taste in poetry as a universal truth.

> You made a mistake: a great part of it is in blank verse: now there is only one measure in English that can be used without rhyme and make genuine verse, the ordinary 10 syllable heroic to wit, and there is only one man living who can write that with success, that is Tennyson. Thompson (1955)877

This is the best support he can offer to a proletarian poet who begs him for help. Fred was later arrested in the famous Norwich riot, 'The Battle of Ham Run' in 1887 and subsequently tortured on the treadmill. Morris goes on to reveal how basic his lack of appreciation of working-class culture really is:

> Now language is utterly degraded in our daily lives, and poets have to make a new tongue each for himself: before he can even begin his story, he must elevate his means of expression from the daily jabber to which centuries of degradation have reduced it. And this is given to few to be able to do. ibid. p.879

From this lambasting of oral language and dialect he goes on to recommend that Fred study Homer and Beowulf. Fortunately, Fred was not easily deterred and in the late 1880s his first volume of poetry was an immediate success. We should note that Thompson does not record the title of his book. These attitudes, made preposterously explicit in these letters, would have been implicit and unspoken in his many circles of influence.

The section on his letters to Fred Henderson, although revealing his attitude to aesthetics and class, is left out of the later editions of E.P Thompson's biography. This is a pattern I have noticed in other books. Slight breaks with good taste occur in first editions, which might have escaped the attention of chief editors. The success of the book then presumably brings it to the attention of the publishers and it is intuitively tidied up for the second or subsequent editions. The point of quoting at length from E.P Thompson is to show how historians can record such classist attitudes without comment and, apparently, without awareness. This is not to decry the later works of Thompson, which are milestones in creating a history from below.

News of Nothing

The socialist utopian tract *Looking Backward* by Edward Bellamy was published in 1888 and quickly assumed an authoritative status, bringing many in the middle classes to socialist positions. Socialism was to be a redemption for their capitalist sins, and an expiation of their guilt: 'He offered his middle-class listeners immediate redemption by the acceptance of socialism.' Meier (1978)39

> To Bellamy, a kindly, academic man, not actively associated with the movement of the working-class, all this violence, greed and selfish conflict was extremely distasteful. It was untidy and unreasonable, it was the tidiness and reason of socialism that most appealed to him. Its triumph, therefore, would be a triumph of abstract reason, not of a revolutionary class. Morton (1952)

There was a deep middle-class desire for purification and cleanliness. The middle class had risen from the dirt of the working-class and feared that any reappearance of dirt might drag them back. I have even heard Fabian socialism summed up as a form of social hygiene.

Morris was repelled by the crude military and centralised aspects of the utopia described by Bellamy and decided he must do better. He immediately started work on *News from Nowhere,* which began to appear as a serial in The Commonweal on January 11th 1890. Bluntly put, Morris wanted a romantic feudal style of socialism. As with the medieval nobility the means of escape from the misery of life lay in 'the way of dream and illusion.' Huizinga (1919)81. He never understood the excitement of the quality of life in cities. Nor did he appreciate the aesthetics and potentially liberating aspects of mass production.

> Being unable to talk to them about themselves, and about reality as they knew it, he was left with only the prospects offered by utopias. Meier (1978)41

The characters in *Earthly Paradise* have been criticised as shadows or fairy-story archetypes. The characters in *News from Nowhere* are certainly cardboard cut-outs. Morris detested realism: 'The men are handsome, strong, attentive and amorous, everybody looks younger than his age and women of forty have not a single wrinkle.' Berneri (1950)260. Even the English weather becomes eternally fine and warm.

News from Nowhere did reach a much wider audience than the usual socialist propaganda. The socialism it promoted replaced industrialism with a rural vision. It captured the Arcadian ideal of the era and gave it a socialist costume. These utopian visions were libertarian compared with others who believed in an overtly paternalist state which was to be the perfect father to the innocent and primitive working-class children. The paternalism of Morris was not so crude, and so his persuasive and charming vision was perhaps even more insidious. He appealed in the most reasonable way for 'a decent life' in the workshop and home before the provision of the public libraries, museums and picture galleries favoured by municipal socialists like the Webbs.

Nonetheless this decent life did not imply working-class liberation in any practical sense and he and his fellow socialists were 'mapping their own personal desires onto a generalised image of the working class.' Waters (1990)64

> George Duveau in his *Sociologie de l'Utopie,* incidentally remarks that there are, with very rare exceptions, no workers' utopias. In fact, if we restrict ourselves to the study of English literature, we are obliged to admit that, from St Thomas More to the most recent writers, utopias have always been a bourgeois phenomenon. Meier (1978)27

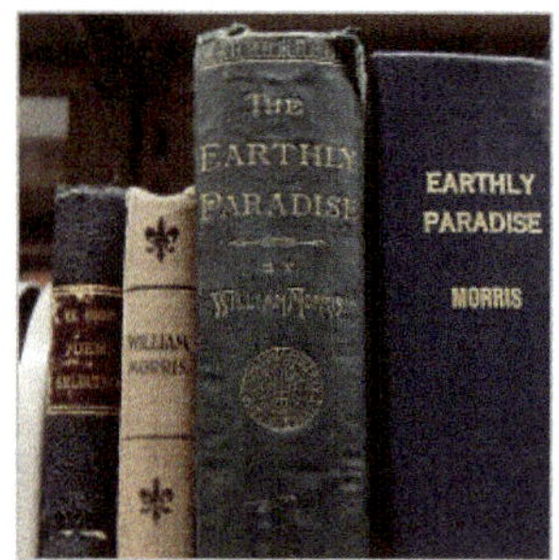

Photography by Romana Klee 2012

Whereas Morris gave us a banal goal but no way to get there, what we need is the concrete techniques of liberation without preconceptions about where this will lead. All visions of heaven have been empty and dull or absurd and fantastical. However, the process of actively emerging from the confusion of oppression towards a greater clarity and rationality of human relations is exciting, requiring a leap into the unknown.

He wanted the working-class to 'free themselves from masters and do it themselves'; but the vision he offered was like a beacon shining in the wrong direction, like a road sign that has been turned to direct us down a cul-de-sac. It was his vision of and for his own class. It was ultimately the values of his class that he wished the workers would take as their values. He lectured them and marveled at their wretched state, but he did not take the time to listen to them or really join them in struggle. He suggested diversionary fantasies and not real productive possibilities. It is important to distinguish between keeping the bigger picture in view in our individual struggles, and being utopian.

> Though we are in many ways familiar with the thought of the utopias of the nineteenth century, they are nevertheless more foreign to us than those of the more distant past. In spite of the fact these utopian writers were no doubt inspired by the highest motives, one cannot help 'feeling bitter about the nineteenth century', like the old man in 'News from Nowhere', bitter even about the love these utopian writers lavished on humanity, for they seem like so many over-affectionate and overanxious mothers who would kill their sons with attention and kindness rather than let them enjoy one moment of freedom. Berneri (1950)

Middle-Class Liberation?

In his correspondence Morris does briefly enter into the middle-class position in oppression. 'They themselves suffer from the same system... their lives made barren and dull by it.' Thompson (1955)176. He never saw that middle-class people were the problem. Ernest Belfort Bax, the philosopher in The League, seemed to be groping for insights into the sham and hypocrisy which was so much part of the middle-class

Victorian family. He complained how the Victorian citizen could be outraged by damage to property, whilst starvation was considered as the natural order of things. Morris simply didn't think any further about how class oppression affected his own class. He took on the easier path of advising others or escaping into fantasy.

Morris hated the work of Aubrey Beardsley, whose work did address middle-class decadence and the manners of oppressors. Until Linda Zatlin's feminist reappraisal, the establishment view was that whilst Beardsley's style was to be admired, the content was to be deplored. She argues that:

> Beardsley's 'protest was not merely an advocacy of sexual education and sexual exploration, but also a disapproval of social hypocrisy and the sexist social conventions which foisted that hypocrisy. ... When Beardsley drew men, he unclothed their lust for power over women. ... When he drew women, he portrayed their intelligence and their sexuality, in bold defiance of Victorian convention.' She argues that he exposes; 'the dependence of most men on money, intellectual coercion and sex for their identity as males and his approbation of a masculinity not contingent on the exploitation of others. Zatlin (1990)

He was obsessed with observing the acquisition of wealth, the coercion of aspiring artists to conform, and men's power over women and their objectification. It is perhaps not surprising that Beardsley's drawings were criticised as ugly and were at the time perceived as a threat to good taste, whilst the work of Morris was about a refinement of good taste.

In 1891 the Morris household at Kelmscott had six servants expected to work very hard for their six to nine pounds per year. We do not hear this from Morris himself, in spite of his voluminous writings and 'class consciousness', but from one who entered service with him about this time, Floss Gumer. It is by such omissions and silences that our image of both Morris and ourselves is distorted.

Health and Emotion

The characteristics of oppressor culture are typified by the stiff upper lip:

the control of emotional discharge. With his typical elegant lucidity, Morris found a clever way to put this so it sounded most reasonable.

> So, it is a point of honour with us not to be self centred, not to suppose that the world must cease because one man is sorry; therefore we should think it foolish, or if you will, criminal, to exaggerate these matters of sentiment and sensibility ... So, we shake off these griefs in a way which perhaps the sentimentalists would think contemptible and unheroic, but which we think necessary and manly. Meier (1978)216

> 'Manly, unmanly' - these are words as important in Morris's vocabulary as `hope'... Man ought to be the master of his emotions, not their victim. Thompson (1955)205

> The first act of violence that patriarchy demands of males is not violence towards women. Instead patriarchy demands of all males that they engage in acts of psychic self-mutilation, that they kill off the emotional part of themselves. If an individual is not successful in emotionally crippling himself, he can count on patriarchal men to enact rituals of power that will assault his self-esteem. bell hooks (2004)

The point is; do we 'master' our emotions by repressing their expression? I would readily agree that it is at times appropriate to regulate their expression, to be in control of when we express emotions, but this is very different from their wholesale repression. Also, although we need to base our actions on our thinking rather than our emotion, this should not imply that the expression of emotion has no place or function.

We find in Thompson's account evidence which suggests that the denial of this aspect of our physicality may have been an important factor in the breakdown in Morris's health.

> In February, 1891, Morris's health collapsed. More than once before attacks of gout had followed hard upon the heels of some disappointment, and it is reasonable to connect this most serious illness of all with the failure of the League and a new turn for the worse of the condition of his daughter, Jenny. Thompson

(1955)671

> I was thinking ... how I have wasted the many times I have been 'hurt' and (especially of late years) have made no sign, but swallowed down my sorrow and anger, and nothing done! Whereas if I had gone to bed and stayed there for a month or two and declined taking any part in life ... I can't help thinking it might have been very effective. Perhaps you remember that this game was tried by many of the Icelandic heroes, and seemingly with great success. ibid. p. 720

Later as his illness progressed and he became weaker the emotions repeatedly broke through his manly veneer of self-control: ‘In his weakness, his strong emotional control was relaxed. When 'Georgie' had said something of the life of the poor, he broke into tears.’ ibid. p. 727. As R.D Laing, the radical Scottish psychiatrist has said, 'The breakdown can be the breakthrough', but for Morris perhaps, the tears came too late and soon after, on the 3rd October 1896, he died.

Cecil Sharp

The Colonisation of British Working-class Song.

Cecil Sharp followed in the footsteps of a long line of folk song collectors and publishers, but it is his name we associate with the category 'folk music.' Cecil Sharp House, the centre of The English Folk Song & Dance Society, is in Camden Town, London, and is still known as the headquarters of English folk music. To understand why Sharp occupies this dominant position we should first look briefly along the line of song mediators that preceded him, picking out a few of the key collectors.

The Earlier Collectors

Broadsides of popular songs were produced from around 1550 and forty or so publishers of broadside song existed in England by the later C17th. The growth of the publishing industry was a key force in the development of capitalism and in the formation of the modern nation state. Books held and disseminated the discourses, knowledge and values that were key to the new bourgeois culture. The dominant worldview was literally that which was published. Silent reading only began in the seventeenth century. Gradually poets began to write for silent reading and the transition from an oral to a literary culture had begun in earnest.

The power of a capitalist depends on the size of his market. Publishing created standardised languages of literacy, which gradually withdrew from the diversity of oral languages and dialects that could be found in the same territory. Literary language and became the language of power. This entirely new type of language embodied the values of the dominant class and defined the geographical area of a nation. We still observe the differences between the old spoken dialects of England and 'Standard English', the official administrative language that most publications appear in. There has been a gradual imposition of this standardised version of the English language and its accompanying set of cultural values, on the whole population. Significantly, 'four letter' words are still remnants of the old Anglo-Saxon oralacy. In my youth, the Catholic mass was still intoned in Latin, which was the language of the European literati when publishing began in the sixteenth century. So, we can see how gradual and layered are these processes of change.

Ambrose Phillips had been to Cambridge University and ended his life as a judge. He was one of the first antiquarians to publish the lyrics of songs with his *Collection of Old Ballads* in 1723. This made a tasteful selection from the popular song of the period including material taken from 'common tradition'. It is from this time that we can trace the myth that the 'better' working-class music, the ballad, was a relic of the minstrels of the medieval age who wandered between noble courts. Imagined as a 'golden age' from which the ancestors of the new middle-classes liked to think they had come. Ballads had been passed on through the generations but had often, so the myth went, degenerated in the hands of the illiterate and vulgar common people. From these 'spoilt fragments' it was fair game for the collector to reconstruct a version which was to be more 'truthful' to the romantically imagined original. As the minstrels were wandering, and hence gathering songs from all regions, it was presumed that they gave the English a homogeneous national culture. According to Dave Harker (1985), Phillips was advised that his first edition was not tasteful enough and he was careful to see to it that his second edition contained; ‘no vile Conceit, no Low Pun, or double Entendre’.

Joseph Ritson had been born in humble circumstances in Stockton-on-Tees in 1752. He had gone to London, done well in business and had become High Bailiff-of-the-Liberty-of-the-Savoy before being called to the Bar. He was strongly anti-aristocratic and had adopted republican views. He took various members of the literary establishment to task, including song collectors like Bishop Percy and John Pinkerton, challenging inaccurate presentations, which he saw as being practically fraud. Bishop Percy's publication of 45 ballads in 1765, *The Reliques,* had challenged the cold formalism of English poetry and influenced people such as Sir Walter Scott, William Wordsworth and Samuel Taylor Coleridge.

In 1783 Joseph Ritson's *A Select Collection of English Songs* set new standards of accuracy for collectors. By the time of the publication, in 1790, of his *Ancient Songs from the Time of King Henry the Third to the Revolution,* there was already a realisation that the formation of a national culture, which reflected a recognisable appearance of common culture without expressing its interests, was useful in bringing the public towards a political unity and loyalty to the state.

Although Ritson accused people such as Bishop Percy of forgery, his own selections were still chosen not to 'tinge the cheek of delicacy, or offend the purity of the chasest ear.' So, whilst Ritson is notable and progressive in bringing increased accuracy to the songs in his collection, by excluding whole songs he critically misrepresented a culture. He had accepted the fiction that 'National Song' was derived from courtly culture, and that the song culture of the common people was a debased remnant of an earlier minstrelsy. The implication was that common people were incapable of creating culture of their own.

It should also be noted that his idea of accuracy was dependent on the market for which he published. He would still correct spellings and grammar and 'make sense of nonsense'. In the process of this translation of oral material to literary English much of the quality of the originals must have been lost. However, it is largely because the different collectors competed with each other over the crucial issue of authenticity, generating a critical discourse around issues of accuracy, that we can get quite a good picture of how the texts were manipulated.

The question of authenticity was important because of the underlying claim on history. If you could convince your reader that your songs represented the true ancient lineage, they could be considered part of a national heritage. If they were proved fraudulent, this whole project fell apart. Authenticity was a key issue in the creation of the nationalist myth but because of the respectable and refined taste of the readership, vulgarity was, paradoxically, unacceptable. This exposes an interesting contradiction that goes to the heart of class oppression. Fundamentally, dominant culture is a repression of the 'lower senses'. The dominant classes, imagining themselves as being more akin to gods than animals, found references to bodily functions repulsive.

Robert Burns was born in 1759 in Alloway, the son of a poor ploughman. He gained an early reputation as a witty poet and songwriter and by 1786 he was being lionized by Edinburgh society. At the same time his poetry sold widely and fulfilled a deep need for the expression of the Scots' identity. Burns was instrumental in the production of the comprehensive six-volume *The Scots Musical Museum,* published in 1803. Driven by a fierce partisan feeling for his downtrodden Scottish brethren, he had given up his own career and spent much of his time from 1787 researching this collection of 600 Scottish songs.

Such an ambitious edition was only possible because of the growing middle-class book-buying market. Although there is no doubt that he recognised the vitality of workers' culture, there was of course considerable pressure on him to make a publication that complied with the edicts and taboos of bourgeois taste. At one point, he admitted that in a 'good many of them, little more than the chorus is ancient, though there is no need for telling everybody this piece of intelligence.' Harker (1985)36. In other words, Burns realised it would spoil his readers' fantasy of it as their own ancient heritage, if he acknowledged authorship. He would also translate texts into educated English with his middle-class audience in mind, typically leaving out all erotic material. Paradoxically it is now only this erotic material that survives unchanged to give us an idea of what the original transcriptions were like. Other collectors would not have even collected erotic material, but it can be seen how the demands of the marketplace of the time made Burns change what he recorded. Then again, Robbie Burns was a rare example of a working-class collector and writer and much may be learned of working-class values from his own work.

The historical context must be kept in mind. During this period, the bourgeoisie was still a new class. Compared to the aristocracy they had little history of their own. They needed and probably still felt a connection to a pre-industrial time in which they would still have been part of the people. However, a truthful picture of people's history may have been too painfully in conflict with their current exploitative practices. They therefore took refuge in a romanticised history seen through the screen of aristocratic values. Central to this myth was a soft-focus image of an idyllic life in the country in touch with nature. This was nostalgia with which almost everyone would empathise, especially as urban life was a relatively new phenomenon. This theme is repeated from the seventeenth century, and in time becomes an important part of even socialist aspirations.

Walter Scott was the son of a well-known Edinburgh lawyer, who was the leading song mediator in the next period of 1800 to 1830. He shared King George IV's fear of the emergent urban workers. Around 1810, cheap political pamphlets and chapbooks proliferated in the cities amid widespread signs of the development of a new urban culture. The urban proletariat was considered a dangerous rabble in contrast to the old peasantry, which was by now relatively unthreatening and fragmented. Scott, it should be noted, was a great medievalist whose books influenced the young William Morris. Scott's songbooks built up an idea of the primitive nobility of the peasant and a reverence for their mythologised medieval past. This was set against the vulgar urban proletariat whose culture should be distanced from that of the bourgeoisie. This whole vector of thought also led to the creation of romantic poetry and a place for those from the bourgeoisie who felt they had to take a position critical of the excesses of their own class.

Walter Scott's *Minstrelsy of the Scottish Borde*r was published in 1802 and presented a biased view of Scottish history mainly focusing on chiefs and nobility. Ordinary people appeared only in the entourage of the powerful, or as soldiers or victims of violence. It avoided any sympathy with democratic causes, and helped to reconstruct history to fit in with the most conservative of bourgeois attitudes. Scott wasn't just looking for good songs from the people; they had to come from 'tradition'. So, the penny pamphleteers, broadsides and chapbooks, the germ of a working-class literature, were derided as vulgar and paltry. To have recognised this cheap type of printed matter as a worthwhile source would have given them value, and was against the very basis of his project.

Scott had a wide circle of helpers and collectors. They all tended to depersonalise and generalise their sources, rarely giving credit to an individual, as if there were no individual creativity or invention amongst the common people. They were seen, rather, as poor vehicles for this stuff coming from the ancient springs of humanity. On top of the classism of the gentlemen collectors, there was the likelihood of self-censorship imposed by the singers themselves. Few people would want to risk upsetting a local gentleman or posh stranger with a song revealing expressions of class anger or violence, which might lead to retribution.

Before Scott died, he admitted that perhaps he was wrong to 'improve the poetry' at the expense of its 'simplicity'. The mother of Hogg, one of his main lower-class collaborators, told him to his face:

> Ye hae spoilt them awthegither. They were made for singin' an' no for readin'; but ye hae broken the charm noo, an' they'll bever be sung mair. An' the worst thing of a', they're nouther richt spell'd nor richt setten down. Harker (1985)70

I particularly like this quote from Harker's book because it gives the rare insight that working-class people were quite aware of what was going on.

Robert Chambers, a middle-class Scot, was the first to address the 'general reader' with his cheap edition of' *The Scottish Ballads,* published in 1829. Chamber's philosophy was 'social progress within sound constitutional limits'. This signaled both a break from the literary antiquarian market and from noble patrons. It also meant that the collections originally formed for owning class audiences were gradually filtering back down to the people. *The Scottish Ballads* was a compilation garnered from other more expensive collections. Chambers would often edit together various versions of a song found in different regions to produce a version that was composed of the best lines and even the best words in each version. As usual, literary or at least commercial merit was gained at the expense of authenticity.

John Broadwood was amongst the collectors busy in the South. Born in 1798, the grandson of a pianoforte manufacturer, his family moved to a C13th estate in Lyne on the Sussex-Surrey border in 1799. In 1851, he succeeded his father as squire. In the meantime, his *Old English Songs* was published in 1843 and it set the tone for the subsequent middle-class folk revival. The book's subtitle is famously long: *Old English Songs: as now Sung by the Peasantry of the Weald of Surrey and Sussex, and collected by one who has learnt them by hearing them Sung every Christmas from early Childhood, by The Country People, who go about to the Neighbouring Houses,*

Singing, 'Waissailing' as it is called, at that Season. The Airs are set to Music, exactly as they are now Sung, to rescue them from oblivion, and to afford a specimen of genuine Old English Melody: and the words are given in their original rough state, with an occasional slight alteration to render the sense intelligible.

He was followed in his mission by his daughter Lucy Broadwood, who was a contemporary of Cecil Sharp. With ever increasing urbanisation and the profound changing relations between owning and labouring classes, 'the people' came under increasing scrutiny. With the rise of the Chartists in the 1830s and 1840s the search for a unifying national cultural heritage was driven by the winds of reaction. The area of study known as folklore developed in this context.

It was thought that 'the golden age of the minstrels' ended in about 1700 after which the ballads were vulgarised by being printed in broadsheets and through oral transmission. The people involved in folklore studies and publishing around the mid-1800s were not state officials or agents but simply people who could afford to follow a genteel hobby. This shows how organically oppression was propagated through a culture of good taste and respectability.

At the same time philanthropists were developing an idea of 'rational recreation'. As organised labour won leisure time the content of this leisure was hotly contested between the dominant culture, with its civilising 'rational recreations', and working-class culture with its own activities, which were represented as 'mindless and frenetic' pleasure-seeking. Commercial popular culture stood in no-man's land ready to exploit whatever yielded a profit in the ensuing battle.

Choral singing became a central part of rational recreation. People were to be brought to respectable socialism by the Vocal Unions. These did not, at this time, focus on the encouragement of traditional song. Montague Blatchford, founder of the Clarion Vocal Union, called for workers to be given an 'art of their own': but this art was to be Tudor madrigals and the like. By the 1880s various prominent agencies were attempting to transform popular culture through the refining qualities of 'good' music. Societies such as the People's Concert Society and the People's Entertainment Society 'were dedicated to destroying worker's ties to 'lower forms of amusement' by training them to a 'very high standard of taste,' which would secure their commitment to the established social order.' Waters (1990)99. The 'lower forms of amusement' referred to were mainly what happened in the public houses and music halls.

> Socialist advocates of choral singing were more concerned with training workers in accepted standards of musical taste than they were in delineating the components of an explicitly socialist culture. Waters (1990)127

Carl Engel, a German émigré, was shocked at the lack of interest taken by British classical musicians in establishing folk roots for their national music, and in 1878, he was pushing for a clear distinction to be made between national and popular. Sabine Baring-Gould, a member of the old English squirarchy, also tried to engage the interest and involvement of professional musicians in the collection of folk material.

As we have seen, collected lyrics were a poor transcription of oral language, and yet clashed with literary standards. The critics had no understanding of the structure of dialect, which was just considered a vulgar version of 'proper' speech and clearly needed to be translated into 'correct' English. Baring-Gould found that 'some of the most exquisite melodies were coupled to either foul or silly words,' or the lyrics were 'Usually rubbish.'

The arrival of Carl Engel with his theories of National Music, and the involvement of the upper-class heavyweight Baring-Gould, signaled the beginning of a new stage in which the music was emphasised over the poetry that Scott and Burns were more interested in. The conscious propagation of an ersatz nationalist identity became increasingly urgent. The working-class folk song culture had been colonised through the activity of the collectors and publishers. It had been cleaned up and was then fused with bourgeois idioms and presented back to the people as the National Culture in opposition to the debased urban popular culture.

The paradoxical situation was that bourgeois culture was in reality internationalist: German symphonies; Italian operas; Russian ballets; French farce. In spite of regional differences and the relative lack of short-term mobility, the people's cultures of Europe and further afield also shared many commonalities. See Bob Pegg, *Rites and Riots*, 1981

Between 1888 and 1915 the word 'folk' was used in the titles of at least 27 song collections. The vast majority of these would be accompanied by piano arrangements:

> While providing the necessary prop for a drawing-room performance and theoretically helping to coordinate the undisciplined singing of a hall full of school children, at the same time imposed the rhythmic strictness and tonal straitjacket of the pianoforte upon a music which appears to have cared not at all for the discipline of the metronome and owed nothing to the chromatic scale employed by art musicians and composers. Pegg (1976)18

The English Folk Song Society, with which Cecil Sharp was to become synonymous, was formed in 1898. Based in London's Mayfair, it attracted leading musical luminaries of the day including the composers Elgar, Dvorak and Grieg. Urban culture was seen as nothing but common rowdyism and sordid vulgarity. Sharp's 'Folksong' was contrasted to the 'glitter, sham and vulgarity' of music hall. It was idealised as unsophisticated, primitive and authentic - simple beauty with common emotion.

Cecil Sharp and the shaping of 20th Century Musical Taste

Cecil James Sharp was born on the 22nd of November 1859, in Denmark Hill, South London, the eldest boy in a family of nine. His father was a slate merchant in Tooley Street, near London Bridge, who had a taste for archaeology and was referred to lovingly by Sharp as 'The General'. His mother was of Welsh and Italian extraction. He was a nervous boy who was 'highly sensitive to noises'. Fortunately, his parents were fond of Handel and Mozart. 'An early and vivid recollection was the sound of a brass band in the street when he was in bed; in his ecstasy, he wept.' Karpeles (1933)4. When he was eight he was sent to a private boarding school in Brighton. At ten he went to Uppingham, the only British public school where music was taken seriously. He entered Cambridge

University in 1879 at the age of 20 to read mathematics, but mostly played the piano. At Cambridge, he was much shaken by Charles Kingsley's *Aalton Locke*, which featured the Chartist monster rally of 10th April 1848, and was influenced by the Christian Socialists. It was here that he first met Charles Marson, an influential figure in Christian Socialism, and the playwright George Bernard Shaw. All three of them later joined The Fabian Society.

Sharp went to Australia in 1882, after graduating from Cambridge, and had jobs which ranged from bank clerk to director of the Adelaide College of Music. Returning in 1892, he got a job as music master at Ludgrove, a preparatory school. The pupils were mainly being prepared for Eton and at one time he was music tutor to the Prince of Wales' children. He stuck at this job until 1910 and this educational experience was to play a major part in his future schemes, but the turning point in his life came with his discovery of folk culture in 1899.

> Sharp and his family spent that Christmas with his wife's mother, who was then living at Sandfield Cottage, Headington, about a mile east of Oxford. On Boxing Day, as he was looking out of the window, upon the snow-covered drive, a strange procession appeared; eight men dressed in white, decorated with ribbons, with pads of small latten-bells strapped to their shins, carrying coloured sticks and white handkerchiefs; accompanying them was a concertina player and a man dressed as a 'fool'. Six of the men formed up in front of the house in two lines of three; the concertina player struck up an invigorating tune, the like of which Sharp had never heard before; the men jumped high into the air, then danced with springs and capers, waving and swinging the handkerchiefs that they held, one in each hand, while the bells marked the rhythm of the step... Sharp watched and listened spellbound. He felt that a new world of beauty had been revealed to him. He had not been well; his eyes had been giving him pain, and he was still wearing a shade over them, but all his ills were forgotten in his excitement. Karpeles (1933)26

He keenly questioned these Morris men, and noted down their tunes. He followed up his interest by looking into the folk song collections of

Kidson and Broadwood, both of whom were members of the English Folk Song Society. By 1902 his newly found enthusiasm had already led him to produce *A Book of British Song for Home and School.* He saw this both as a collection of national song and a collection of ideal texts and tunes. However, it was only in 1903 that he heard his first live folk song, in Hambridge, Somerset.

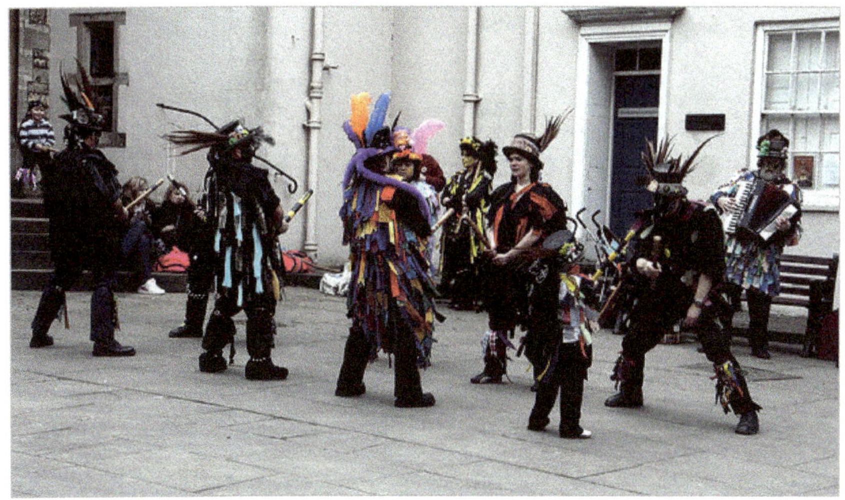

Morris Dancers in Lincoln 2009 photograph by Pete

> That song was 'The Seeds of Love' that was Sharp's introduction to the live folk song. He was sitting in the garden talking to Mattie Kay, and John England was singing quietly to himself as he mowed the lawn. Sharp whipped out his notebook, took down the tune, and afterwards persuaded John to give him the words. He went off and harmonised the song, and that same evening it was sung at a choir supper by Mattie Kay, Sharp accompanying. The audience was delighted; as one said, it was the first time that the song had been put into evening-dress. John was proud, but doubtful about the 'evening-dress'; there had been no piano to his song. Karpeles (1933)33

Mattie Kay was Sharp's demonstration singer. In the revised edition of Maud Karpeles biography published in 1967, the revealing last sentence is edited out. The following quote on Sharp's collecting is also cut:

> I was in her wash-house sitting on an inverted tub, notebook in hand, while my hostess officiated at the copper, singing the while. Several neighbours congregated at the door to watch the strange proceedings. In one of the intervals between the songs one of the women remarked, 'You be going to make a deal o' money out o' this, sir?' My embarrassment was relieved by the singer at the washtub, who came to my assistance and said, "Oh! It's only 'is 'obby". "Ah! Well," commented the first speaker, "We do all 'ave our vailin's". Karpeles (1933)36

This is another rare insight into the cynical attitude that some working people had towards the motives of the collectors - their awareness that all was not well with the process they were witnessing.

Sharp had found his mission in life. He had long felt that English culture, since Purcell, was lacking a native idiom. All was imported. He had been looking for the roots of a national culture and now all the pieces were coming together. He used his media connections to get publicity for his ideas into the Morning Post. With the other prominent collectors Broadwood, Baring-Gould and Marson, he then took control of the English Folk Song Society. The four of them pooled their contacts and considerable influence to popularise these ideas. 'Our traditional songs are a great instrument for sweetening and purifying our national life and for elevating and refining popular taste.' Harker (1985)183

Working-class culture was to be stultified, backdated, modified, cleaned up and sold back to us as the genuine article - the mythologising of authenticity that goes to the irrational core of bourgeois culture. This was to be done by infecting one of the great hopes of working people, education.

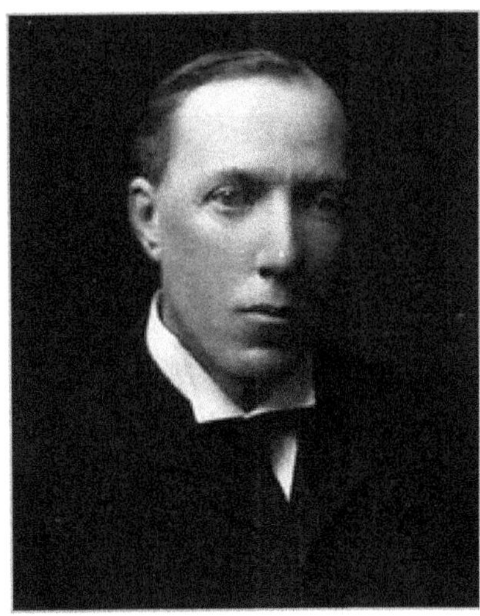

Cecil Sharp Photograph c1900

Song - The Perfect Vehicle of Indoctrination

Since 1840, the state had taken an increasing interest in the education of children. By about 1880 John Hullah had structured singing lessons within the strict harmonic code favoured by the established order. His Tonic Sol-fa method was taken up by schools.

> The Tonic Sol-fa system of music notation was originally intended as a means of moral training for workers, giving the illusion of unsupervised participation without threatening middle-class cultural hegemony. Although socialists used Tonic Sol-fa notation, the equation of the system with the improvement of musical aptitude within well-defined boundaries, made it hard for socialists to overcome its conservative connotations. In short, while they demanded that workers help construct a socialist culture, socialists hoped to develop workers' consciousness of this need by using methods that, by definition, could subvert their own goals. Waters (1990)128

William Chappell was another song collector and writer, whose father sold pianos and sheet music from a shop in Bond street. The mass production of cheap pianos helped the dissemination of these ideas. The result was that collected music became disfigured by harmonies. The collection of tunes, within the strict code of musical notation, reduced them to precise and limited conventions. Subtle variations of pitch and timing where lost. Some tunes would lose all their life when converted into written music.

The 'high moral tone', which was applied to censor the content of songs, became part of the Victorian manufacture of childhood. The vulnerability of the young was confused with a myth of innocence. The reasonable protection of children from abuse was confused with a protection from supposedly crude language and vulgar realities: in other words, from working-class language and culture. Every child attending free state education was to be inculcated from the start with 'good taste'. So as young people were released from the bondage of child labour they were embraced by a new style of oppression.

I remember the relief with which I looked forward to the break from the harsh daily regime of my Roman Catholic junior school to sing-along with the BBC radio once a week. I loved the little songbooks, handsomely illustrated with woodcuts or pen and ink drawings, which were, like school milk, supplied free. Notably they were the only publications we were allowed to take home and keep for ourselves. I still have several copies of *'Singing Together: Rhythm and Melody, BBC Broadcasts to Schools'*, from the late fifties.

At the end of the nineteenth century the movement for public secondary education was on the march, fueled by an increasingly technocratic industry and the perceived need to inculcate time thrift and punctuality.

> In 1907 article 20 of the Regulations stated that the proportion of free places [to Grammar Schools] 'will ordinarily be 25 per cent of the scholars admitted' ... The scholarship Regulations of 1907 were thus a vital part of the ladder of opportunity between the elementary school and the grammar school and a step on the way towards secondary education for all. Sanderson (1987)24

In the same year Sharp produced his key book of theory, *English Folksong: Some Conclusions.* The expansion of state-organised mass education was exactly the vehicle of indoctrination that the national culture-mongers needed. The Board of Education had in 1906, already issued a report which suggested the school curriculum should include 50 'National or Folk Songs' - 'The expression in the idiom of the people of their joys and sorrows, their unafflicted patriotism'. Sharp wanted only 'pure' folk song:

> Let the Board of Education introduce the genuine traditional song into the schools and I prophesy that within the year the slums of London and other large cities will be flooded with beautiful melodies, before which the raucous, unlovely and vulgarising music-hall song will flee as flees the night mist before the rays of the morning sun. Sharp, Correspondence (V), 3.4.1906

> We may look therefore, to the introduction of folk-songs in the elementary schools to effect an improvement in the musical taste of the people, and to refine and strengthen the national character. The study of the folk-song will also stimulate the growth of the feeling of patriotism. It cannot be said that, in the present moment, the English people are remarkable for their love or pride of country.

> There are many ways of stimulating the feeling of patriotism. Education is one of them. Our system of education is, at present, too cosmopolitan; it is calculated to produce citizens of the world rather than Englishmen. And it is Englishmen, English citizens that we want.

> If every English child be placed in possession of all these race products, he will know and understand his country and his countrymen far better than he does at present; and knowing and understanding them he will love them the more, realise that he is united to them by the subtle bond of blood and kinship, and become, in the highest sense of the world, a better citizen, a true patriot. The discovery of the English folk-song, therefore, places in the hands of the patriot, as well as the educationalist, an instrument of great value. The introduction of folk-songs into our schools will not only affect the musical life of England; it will tend also to arouse that love of country and pride of race, the absence of which we now deplore. Sharp (1907)135-36

Dirty Songs

> The subjects of the folk-ballads, that are sung in different parts of Europe, are substantially the same. Some of them have been traced to an Eastern origin, and they all appear to have been drawn from a common storehouse, the heritage, presumably, of the Aryan race. Sharp (1907)89

Sharp romanticised 'the common people' and criticised his bourgeois colleagues who conflated this idea with the modern masses, those who 'confound the common language of the illiterate with the dialect of the unlettered, and refuse to distinguish between the instinctive music of the common people and the debased street-music of the vulgar.' Sharp (1907)33

This way of sounding radical, populist, even progressive, when you are essentially being reactionary and elitist is certainly something I recognise as the behaviour of the art establishment of my own time. For a young working-class intellectual, there is a deep unease that is difficult to put your finger on. At times this unease is even felt as a deep revulsion, which all too often leads to a general disillusionment with everything intellectual or arty.

At the same time as going on about authenticity, Sharp's actual practice when collecting was far from objective. He would only record words at all if he approved of their quality. This hypocrisy was built into the typical Victorian family. Here is Mary Neal, a one-time colleague of Sharp, describing her own family: 'Typical of the Victorian age: everything must be correct on the surface, no matter what the reality.' Quoted by Judge (1989)

Of course, the quality of listening and the gesturally communicated interest of the listener will affect what people come out with, what they complete and how they perform.

> Henry Burstow, who claimed to know four hundred songs, would not sing much of his repertoire, 'unfit for ladie's ears' as it was, while another man had many songs he would not sing 'even to a gentleman'. Pegg (1976)14

So-called 'dirty' songs were the first to go. They would rarely have been sung in the presence of a gentleman. Jerry Silverman puts it succinctly in the introduction to his collection, *The Dirty Song Book*:

> Where were the folksong collectors when the dirty songs were being sung? Where were the dirty songs when Cecil Sharp, Carl Sandburg and John Lomax came around? How is it that in song after song, unearthed and preserved by these and other scholars, sexual references, when they do exist, are smoothed over and couched only in the vaguest of terms? ...Did the cowboy, sailor, or chain gang convict suddenly become shy when confronted with the strange fellow with the notebook (and much later the tape-recorder)? Or did the collector himself bowdlerize, expurgate, edit - and in short, 'clean up' priceless and irretrievable examples of the natural wit, candour and insight of his informants' songs?
>
> And yet dirty songs have always been sung. They exist in the oral tradition and are preserved through the folk process. They surface in schools, camps, military service, pubs and in so many other natural gathering places where singing plays a role that we can only infer a tacit conspiracy of silence as the reason for their almost complete nonexistence in print ...when Alec Guiness led his hardy band over the River Kwai they only whistled the tune of the so-called 'Colonel Bogey's March'. Do you suppose that the British soldiers didn't have some choice lyrics to fit that stirring march? Your're damned right they did! Turn to page 92 for a poetical analysis of the anatomy of Hitler, Goering, Himmler and Goebbels and then see if you could ever be satisfied just whistling the tune again. Silverman (1985)

Music Hall

The music hall was the commercial side of the mediation of working-class culture. It had grown from tavern singsongs:

> 'Everyone free and easy...
>
> Do as you damn well pleasey...'

The people present in a public house each took a turn at singing a song or whatever they fancied to entertain the company. In one club, people who did not sing would have to drink a pint of salty water as a forfeit. These Free 'n' Easies then gradually became formalised with professional acts and an entrance fee. By the 1850s they were further formalised by moving into purpose-made theatres. These proved so popular that by 1870 there were at least 415 music halls in Britain.

> Over the course of the Nineteenth century, the 'audience', once taking it in turns to do an act, came to be 'sedated' in fixed seating and more of a spectatorate. The performer, once hardly distinguishable from the audience in the days of the free and easy in a pub, came to be a syndicated artist for a limited liability company, and a worker who needed trade union protection like any other with a capitalist employer.

> The selection had to be made from the cultural stock generated by the working-class. The triumph of the Empire over the Effingham Arms ensured that the view of life selected for projection (even if it was never totally or even deeply assimilated) would be that of the satisfied customer, rather than the angry producer - a culture of consolation rather than confrontation! Penelope Summerfield in Yeo (1981)

> There was no abrupt terminus to music hall's career but its problems were now more than those of outfacing puritans without and unionists within. By 1912 music hall was well into a crisis of over production and reduced profits. Bailey (1986)

By the time Sharp was writing his book *Some Conclusions* in 1907 the music hall had passed the peak of its commercial success.

> Up until now the street song has had an open field; the music taught in the schools has been hopelessly beaten in the fight for supremacy. But the mind that has been fed on the pure melody of the folk will instinctively detect the poverty-stricken tunes of the music hall, and refuse to be captivated and deluded by their superficial attractiveness. Good taste is, perhaps, largely a matter of environment; but it is also the result of careful and early

training. Sharp (1907)135

> Flood the streets, therefore, with folk-tunes and those, who now vulgarise themselves and others by singing coarse music hall songs, will soon drop them in favour of the equally attractive but far better tunes of the folk. This will make the street a pleasanter place for those who have sensitive ears, and will do incalculable good in civilising the masses. ibid. p.137

Dance and Mary Neal

Sharp also collected and promoted folk dances, especially The Morris. In this area, he was initially led by Mary Neal, a powerful and good-hearted philanthropist. She was looking for dances to introduce to her Settlement Club for working girls and had asked Sharp for advice. He knew little about dances at this time, but told her of his experience at Headington and gave her the name of one of the dancers, William Kimber. 'She promptly took a train to Oxford and a hansom cab to Headington Quarry where she found William Kimber and arranged for him and his cousin to come to London to teach dances to the girls.' Judge (1989). It is interesting that Headington was the site of prolonged and riotous resistance to an enclosure between 1850 to 1890.

The women taught by Kimber were then invited to teach classes themselves. The fashion for the folk revival was taking off and soon they were in demand all over the country. Mary Neal had her own strong ideas about folk dance which she promoted with her Esperance Troupe. One of the most central tenets of her philosophy was that dances should be learnt, wherever possible, direct from a traditional dancer. She promoted The Morris as vigorous, joyful and easy to learn. Sharp was her colleague for the first two years but then began to realise that her ideas were leading on the one hand to a romantic excess of the 'Merrie England' sort and on the other were too close to the qualities of working-class culture and that Mary Neal threatened his project and his leadership. He decided that he must regain control. Frantically, he began to collect dances, publishing them in a series of books. In this way, he built up his authority in the proper literary manner. Mary on the other hand believed that the dances should stay in the minds of the dancers! Sharp also began to train teachers, and from his group of 'Chelsea girls' formed a demonstration team. Using his professional educator's base and contacts, he campaigned for a professionalised approach to the teaching of Morris. He set standards and believed the dances should be preserved, recorded and taught in the 'purest form'.

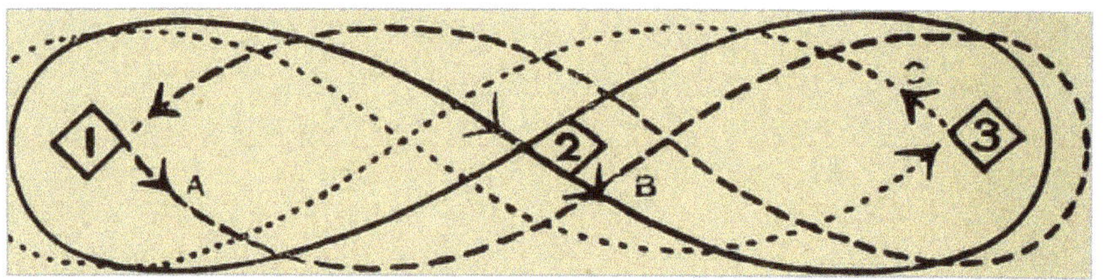

Diagram from 'The Country Dance Book' by Karpeles, Butterworth and Sharp, 1909

At the same time, although Mary Neal was less Machiavellian than Sharp, she was a better organiser and her movement was continuing to proliferate. From about 1910 Sharp attacked the performances of the Esperance as execrable, debased, hoydenish, over-strenuous, undignified, uncouth, too flamboyant and decorative, and altogether a gruesome spectacle. She on the other hand called him a pedant and their hatred for each other grew. Here is Mary Neal describing Sharp's troupe:

> The atmosphere, the movements, the general style of the dancing is not that inspired by the peasant mind, the uncultured, unlettered artist of the field; it is rather the adaptation of this by the cultured musician.

She contrasted this with a traditional performance at Bampton:

> The men danced in a sort of trance, in a mood inarticulate, unselfconscious; each man had his own way with the steps, no two dancing precisely alike, and yet the same mood was so heavy upon all that the general effect was harmonious and curiously impressive. Judge (1989) quoting from The Observer 3.12.1911

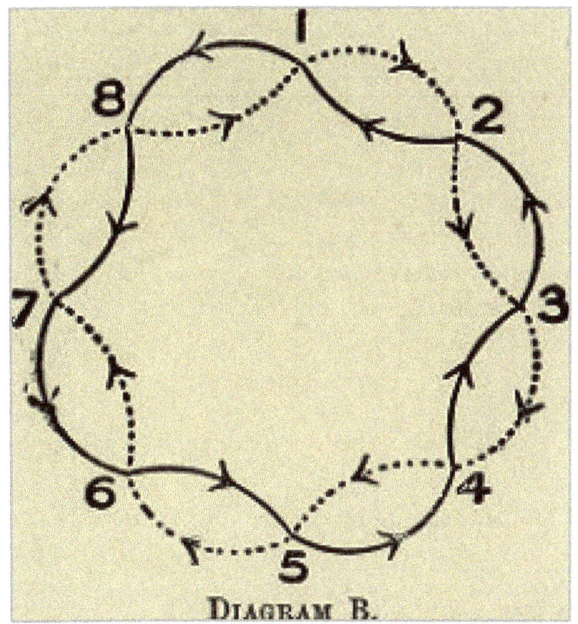

DIAGRAM B.

On another occasion Neal pointed out the difference in class between her dancers and Sharp's who she thought demonstrated the inability of 'the average young lady or gentleman to get near to the spirit of the dance.' Her own dancers, 'working lads and lasses, from town and country,' did, she thought, more closely achieve this spirit.

> Like the Victorian and Edwardian folk-song collectors, who selected songs according to quite personal and unscientific standards, the early chroniclers of country dance chose their material in a way which, while not totally arbitrary, did not reflect the taste of the people they collected from. Pegg (1976)108

World War 1 interrupted activity and afterwards the Esperance Club was never reformed, perhaps because Neal had realised, in a devastating moment, that The Morris was essentially a male ceremonial. However, Sharp's institutionalised position had gained ascendancy and survived the war.

Both Neal and Sharp misunderstood and appropriated the Morris. Sharp's motives were more 'elevated' and his understanding of the function of good taste in the task of mediation more thorough. His was the exemplary 'rational' approach of the dominant culture. Neal, an active supporter of women's suffrage, perhaps understood things too much from the other side of the coin.

In the years before the War, Sharp, with the help of his influential friends was already pulling most of the strings in the folk song and dance movement. The president of the English Folk Dance Society was now a friend of his from Australia; Lady Mary Trefusis, who was 'Woman of the Bedchamber to Queen Mary', and by the end of 1913 Sharp could announce that: 'Speaking from memory, I should say that the majority of our certificate holders are elementary school teachers!'

> Well before the State recognition, which followed the end of the war, Sharp had built up his folk-dance cadre, and had permeated the plutocratic part of the movement with Webbian efficiency. Harker (1982)

Whose Culture?

By 1913 Fabians had made an alliance with the Labour Party and Sharp had to be persuaded to rejoin by Beatrice Webb. 'It was felt we had to take some part in the organisation of the Labour Party, as perhaps the most potent instrument for permeating working-class opinion.' Sharp Correspondence, 7.5.1913

After 1917, the time was ripe for turning this bourgeois fad with folk into a 'restoration of heritage' to 'the common herd.' The composer Vaughan Williams explains:

> Country people from whom we get our songs are only a small part of our population - why should their music be essentially our national music? Is it not because it is only there... we can find music in its most primitive state and this is the reason, is it not, why we go to them to find out where our national music really is? Harker (1985)209

This was seen as the embryo of all nationalist culture, an embryo the working-class had abandoned and which it was up to the native composers of the bourgeoisie, as natural leaders of the people, to save and develop. By the end of his life Sharp had, with a prodigious expenditure of energy, collected some 3000 songs in Britain and 1500 in the USA. It is noteworthy that Sharp, writing in 1916, describing John Lomax's *Oral Cowboy Songs and other Frontier Ballads* as 'a volume which contains nothing but the dregs of literature and the garbage of musical phrase.' Sharp in a letter to Mrs Storrow, 6.12.1916

Around 1908 Percy Grainger had collected songs in Lincolnshire with a wax cylinder Edison Bell Phonograph. He repeatedly studied his recordings and began to come to conclusions which challenged the 'folk song consensus'. He noticed the importance of style and variation in the singers' use of harmonic scales which, if proven, would have meant that 'the conventional system of modal classification would have to be scrapped, and the folk-song collections would be seen as no more than artful re-creations for a middle-class public.' Bob Pegg (1976)21

Grainger's observations were published in the Folk Song Society's Journal in 1908. Grainger, who had extreme right-wing ideas, dropped the subject and nobody followed up his work. Machine recording was not used again for collecting in the UK until the work of the BBC in the 1950s. Even then the change to sound recording by collectors was painfully slow. In 1976 Bob Pegg was heard to remark that there was still a complete lack of recorded music from whole areas of the Midlands and the North. These heavily industrialised areas would have promised to reveal a rich continuity of rural folk and urban song.

The explosion of electronic rock music, youth subcultures and records with their large markets overtook the slow-moving folk scene. Music was increasingly being produced for the recording. Making a record was the main object of much music making for the first time. With the arrival of personal computers in the eighties, studio quality recording became possible in the garage of ever Tom, Dick and Harriet. British rock music largely sidestepped the pollution and censoring of our indigenous tradition, and took much of its influence from across the Atlantic - yet there is probably more native influence and continuity with urban musics of the past in our contemporary rock than is generally known.

Now it is mainly commercial considerations and power struggles within the vast pop music industry that limit what rises to public attention through commercial success, although the good taste of the media still has its crucial filtering effect. On top of this the popular cultural taste that informs this market was deeply affected by those processes and values that Sharp had managed to impress on the national psyche through the school system.

In the bleak cultural atmosphere of the London suburbs, the extraordinary and subtly manipulative ritual of the BBC broadcasts to schools was my only contact with a rich tradition of working-class song. Before the Nineteen Fifties the villages and towns of Britain had been alive with song. People would sing at work, after work in a pub, at church on Sunday, on coach trips: life was full of song. In the suburbs of the fifties the tradition had often been almost completely broken. My Grandpa Sid, away up in Nottingham, had played violin in the church orchestra but he never played it at home when we visited. My own attempt to restart was met with a harsh; 'Pity you can't sing!' a judgement which must have been based on the success of the Sol-fa scale and the general message that the working-class people who didn't pick up these conventions quickly, or who intuitively resisted them, 'couldn't sing'. Singing was considered a gift - you either had it or you didn't - rather than something you picked up from those around you. It was a revelation to me when, as a teenager, I visited folk clubs in cellars and barges and heard all kinds of rough-hewn and beautiful voices, whose value was all expression and little to do with the rigid adherence to a convention of notes. Having said that the postwar folk revival was still generally under the sway of Sharp's ideas.

One area in which the tradition survived and thrived in its oral form was as erotic material. It was in the boys' showers in secondary school in the early sixties that I learnt all the rude 'rugby songs', material that the prudish collectors had avoided but which are, by almost any definition, folk songs. See Bob Pegg's book *Folk* (1976), for a good chapter on this.

Does this explain why the resurgence of English working-class music by way of rock 'n' roll was primarily influenced by Afro-American Rhythm 'n' Blues? The fracture of our tradition had been so severe that it was simply unavailable in a form that had sufficient expressive depth.

Our adoption of imported black music shows the persistence of working-class culture that can arise like a phoenix by adopting whatever tradition is available.

It also reminds me of how rock music was attacked when I was a youth and how much my own parents had been convinced that these values were correct and became agents of the oppression. No place was safe from the onslaught, except perhaps late-night R&B clubs which I occupied like some psychic haven. When I first wrote this book, snobbish middle-class people could still occasionally be heard to reiterate the myth that there is only one type of 'good' music. From the time of William Morris good music was assumed to 'elevate the passions and pave the way for social harmony.' Good music promoted morality whilst 'bad' music was a force for immorality. In my youth, I was told not to buy those pop records because they wouldn't last more than a few weeks. Why didn't I buy some 'serious' (i.e. classical) music that had stood the test of time? Rock music was seen as sexually immoral and culturally bankrupt.

This experience will be familiar to most of my generation. What is remarkable is that these myths, generated before the turn of the century, were still going strong sixty or seventy years later and had been internalised by working people like my parents. It shows how successful the mediators were in their undermining of working-class culture and autonomy. How thoroughly they estranged us from our history.

This process by which people's culture is cleaned up, as it is collected or studied, is probably universal to dominant cultures, as suggested by this quote from a South African journal at the end of the Eighties:

> The study of 'freedom songs' has taken a back seat in academic circles. Ethnomusicologists such as the Tracys have collected hundreds of songs but amongst their collections one can't find 'freedom songs'. Social historians have studied a wide variety of topics but hardly ever political songs. The History Workshop has, to my knowledge, only presented two papers which touch on the topic. *Staffrider* (1989)83

In spite of all this, rock and pop music have given expression to an urban culture, sometimes with astounding power in spite of the commercialisation of the industry. The high profits to be made from this market shouted down the fey BBC version of Sharp's national music. If you were a Ted, Mod, Hippy, Punk or Raver who was part of the scene that suddenly found itself leading the market, you experienced a strange and exciting sense of power. For an enchanted moment, you were there directing market forces rather than simply being a victim of them. It is an experience that demonstrates that when working-class culture chooses autonomously, the market has to fall over itself to keep up and recuperate that autonomy. This recuperation was about to devour the rave scene at the time I wrote the first edition (see *Time Out*, July 14-21 (1993)14). It is a potent form of oppression. We are also aware that a consensual working-class culture has an undeniable power and it is up to us to 'fight the power.'

From the Ruins...

At some point in the sixties the bubble that Sharp helped to create burst:

> Around that time a good many of us were getting into folk music. And folk music, through no active fault of its own, fooled us into certain sympathies and nostalgic alliances with the so-called traditional past. The Thirties. The Highways and Open Roads. The Big West, The Southern Mountains. The Blues, Labour Unions, Childe Ballads. All of which left their mark, even on this record. Almost as if Chuck Berry and Batman had really nothing to do with who we were and Uncle Dave Macon or Horton Barker could do a better job of telling us. But the paradox was implicit: what the hell were rebels doing looking around for roots? And how long would people with contemporary poetic sensibilities be content to sing archaic material for an immediate purpose? Especially when their government was in the habit of wrenching them away from their growth to train them as two-year technicians in a nuclear army. The underground reaction, the reaction in the cellars of what you might call everybody's own MacDougal Street, was topical and quick. Richard Farina (1965)

The trouble was that most of us had already become consumers, reduced to humming along with the record.

Bob Pegg defines folk music by hanging it onto the thread of oralacy, but perhaps the key project for a real people's culture is to take on the literary; on our own terms; with our own materials. In the space of a generation or two, an immense wealth of completely new song has accumulated. This includes much 'golden oldie' material that is without much doubt working-class culture. In forty-five years (to 1993) I know what must be many hundreds of excellent tunes and fragments of lyrics.

Then recently, like a rebound from the farthest eastern reaches of rock's sphere of influence, came Karaoke. The increasing passivity that technology seemed to exert was inverted. People could perform songs from the living archive in their own style or as a caricature of the original, sometimes even adding their own words. Karaoke allowed people to develop the confidence to stand up in front of a crowd and express something. Another important thing is that people can read the lyrics for the first time. Karaoke has given us back the lyrics as literature. The words in the original records were not always clear. It can be surprising what comes up on the Karaoke screen. Particularly surprising if the first time you see them is whilst you are performing! This allows a different level of assessment of the song's content to occur and may have yet unknown repercussions beyond an increase in sales of song-books.

There was another unsatisfactory thing about commercial rock and pop. That was the glamorisation of the rock star. This idealisation created an audience of passive consumers. Karaoke allows everyone to be the lead singer. To get the attention which makes performing so thrilling. To stop living vicariously and do it.

Shake it up baby now...

Chapter Postscript: Since writing this in 1993 the 'karaoke' conclusion above has dated. I think that the key route to power we can take when faced with the commodification of music, is to select our own playlists that go beyond the banal range of music played by the commercial radio stations. Add to this is an emphasis on *talking about* the music we select. This thought resulted in my *Agit Disco* project, which may be reissued as an ebook at some point.

Clough Williams-Ellis

How the self-provision of modern working-class housing was suffocated

Clough Williams-Ellis is now best known as the designer of Portmeirion in North Wales, an ersatz holiday village which became used as the set for the cult Sixties TV series *'The Prisoner.'* He is also known, to students of the conservation and ecology movements, for his book *England and the Octopus*. Lewis Mumford wrote the introduction and calls the author a 'master of urbane design' and describes the book, which first came out in 1928, as a testament to his aesthetic ability. Mumford then goes on to say:

> Not even the high eloquence of Ruskin, the suave contempt of Mathew Arnold, to say nothing of the downright castigation of William Morris, could weaken the stranglehold of the many tentacled Octopus whose inky secretions were inimicable to every form of organic life. Mumford (1928)

Clough Williams-Ellis was a charismatic character whose influence was also felt on architecture, particularly in planning control and new town development. From this vantage point Ellis and his colleagues managed to smother working-class initiatives which promised the evolution of a new urban vernacular.

> Architectural taste, like manners, travels downwards. Dyos, (1961)83

The Shanty Houses of Britain

> His piece of land cost him £10 in 1934. It is 40 ft wide by 100 ft deep. First, he put up a tent which his family used at weekends, and he gradually accumulated tools, timber and glass which he

> brought to the site strapped to his back as he cycled down from London. Hardy & Ward (1984)200

In the first half of the twentieth century, and particularly in the inter-war period, up to the 1947 Planning Act, the appearance throughout Britain of thousands of self-built shacks, chalets and shanties was considered by the powers-that-be to be an eyesore. They said they were a 'blot on the landscape' but from another viewpoint, further down the social scale and from the perspective of fifty years hence, they look like the beginning of a new postmodern urban vernacular, a real working-class architecture in the process of being evolved, brought down before it could flower.

The phenomenon had all the signs of something that, if it had only been encouraged rather than suppressed, could have solved our housing crisis from the ground up. Now we have the outrageous injustice of thousands of square feet of buildings lying empty, whilst people are homeless and daily being thrown out of their own homes because they cannot keep up with the mortgage or rental payments. They are often left not only homeless, but hopelessly in debt.

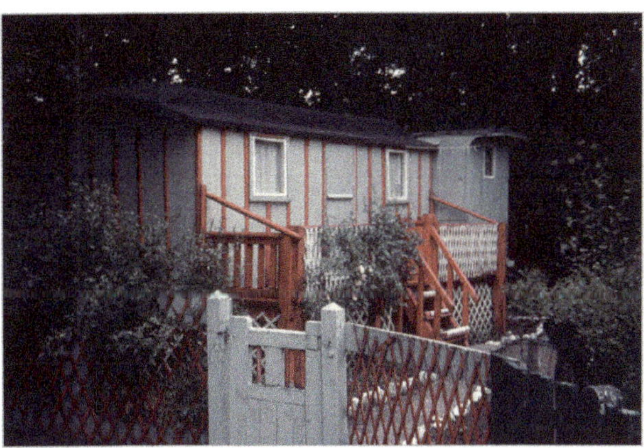

The shanty settlements themselves attracted a large lower-class bohemian element. Artists, writers, actors, music hall and early film stars all found the atmosphere of creativity to their taste.

> One of the celebrities to visit Shoreham Beach was the music hall star, Will Evans, who named a number of the bungalows after pantomimes in which he had appeared - like Cinderella and

> Sleeping Beauty. It was also the scene of early film making, with its own studio and personalities who stayed in the district. Hardy & Ward (1984)92

It is even claimed by an inhabitant of Shoreham Beach, Mrs Cox, that the first colour film was made there. The presence of these cultural workers suggests the shanties were not an isolated phenomenon, but part of a widely based urban working-class culture in the making.

They were encouraged by the back-to-the-land movement which was an aspect of a broad romantically-based Arcadianism fed from many different directions. Writers like William Morris, Prince Kropotkin and Leo Tolstoy created powerful images of future societies without cities. The idea of smallholdings as a solution to unemployment was also supported by radical trade unionists like Ben Tillett and Tom Mann.

> A surprisingly high proportion 'were either socialists or new lifers or both'. Jack David, for example, was an East Londoner who had an office job in the city, was secretary of Marlow Labour Party and was one of the group that published the Socialist Clarion in High Wycombe. George Woodcock quoted remembering his childhood by Hardy & Ward, (1984)180

Free Time

The shanties had different causes in different areas of the country. In the north-east of England families losing their jobs in the mines would find themselves evicted from the tied cottages and having to improvise shelter on their allotment. At one time in the Thirties 32 families were living on the allotments in the Durham mining village of Horden.

The biggest general influence on their development was the winning of leisure time by the organised urban working-class. Disciplining a work force for wage labour had been a long and arduous task. The first generation of factory workers, from around 1700, were seriously oppressed by time. Working fifteen-hour days, they were practically imprisoned in the factories.

The preliminaries to the industrial revolution were so long that,

> in the manufacturing districts in the early 18th century, a vigorous and licensed popular culture had evolved, which the propagandists of discipline regarded with dismay ...the long dawn chorus of moralists is a prelude to the quite sharp attack upon popular customs, sports, and holidays which was made in the last years of the 18th century and the first years of the 19th century. Thompson (1992)

Such an onslaught on people's old working patterns was not, of course, uncontested. By the next generation they were more organised and the Ten-Hour Movement had started. Finally, in 1850 The Ten-Hour Act was passed. Another sixty years of struggle passed before the eight-hour day was generally won in 1919 and this only to placate the survivors of the Great War.

The weekend was another hard-won chunk of free time. In the late seventeenth-century it had become a custom of the more independent manual trades to take Monday off after the Sabbath. This unofficial custom was known as Saint Monday and spread until, by the middle of the nineteenth century, it was widespread. The Bank Holiday Act of 1871 was another milestone. Passed in favour of the banks, it was quickly adopted by industry as a whole.

By 1900 the modern weekend, bank holidays and annual week holiday with pay were commonplace and Charles Booth could comment that holidaymaking 'was one of the most remarkable changes in the last ten years.' The middle classes had already led the fashion of visiting seaside resorts in the first half of the nineteenth century. Now certain resorts such as Blackpool, Southend, Margate and Bridlington became established as working-class resorts. It was around these that some of the first shanties were built to cater for those who perhaps could not afford hotels or boarding houses. The starting point was often an obsolete railway carriage or other industrial container.

However, it was not only coastal areas that attracted the shanty builders. In Shepperton-on-Thames, where I lived from the age of 11 to 18, the shanties are now the most valuable properties in the area, often having sought-after river frontage. Here in the Thames Valley the full force of repression was focused. Place like Eton, Windsor and Henley had been the heartland of the establishment.

> It 'must have seemed the undisputed sanctuary of a privileged caste. So, suddenly to find greengrocers from Acton and printers from Fulham making free with their 'squalid little huts' must have raised blood pressures to dangerous levels ... the ascendance of vulgar, popular culture.' Hardy & Ward (1984)185. (also, Carey (1992)42 + 130)

Now these dwellings have merged into their settings, with matured gardens, and are generally recognised as some of the more interesting examples of riverside architecture.

The Commons Legacy

Following the Norman Conquest there was a massive land reallocation, and following this, a long process of enclosing commons and extinguishing people's rights of access to the land and its products. Common rights are still being usurped and people are still resisting this oppression. The need to have control of the land on which we live, and from which we live, lies deep within each human. The injustice by which this right was taken from the people and the heavy payments imposed on them to get tiny bits of it back should never be forgotten.

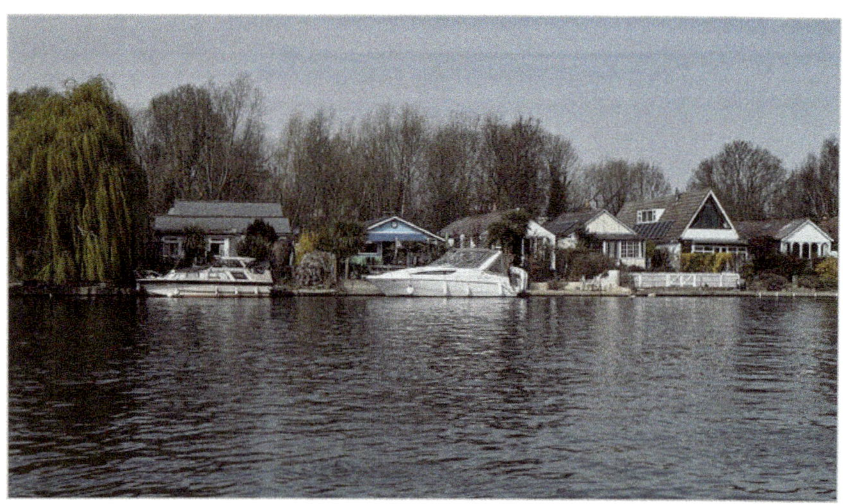

Photography of plotland chalets in Shepperton 2014

This may explain the deep desire I have always felt for land... a place of my own. Leasehold has always seemed unsatisfactory. That we can be made to pay a massive mortgage, for something that still belongs to someone else, seems an unpleasant form of subjugation. Housing is a powerful medium of class oppression:

> In the 19th century the estate planners tried to carefully contain these classes, by allocating special streets for them ... or by moving them out altogether. Muthesius (1982)237

Apart from the planned segregation by street and area, and the obvious hierarchy of size, class distinctions were made through the choice and design of architectural elements. Throughout the Nineteenth century there was an increasingly detailed class differentiation of domestic dwellings. A stifling architectural culture of decorum and propriety drizzled down from the Victorian elite. There was little space in the towns for architectural expression by the working-class. It is not easy to stand back and see the cultural fabric within which you are immersed. Occasionally whilst reading Multhesius' book, *The English Terraced House,* I had a glimpse of just how deadening is the whole phenomenon of urban housing *provision*. On a profound level of cultural expression, it doesn't belong to you. It is something that has been forced upon you. Even if you manage to buy your house, you still live in someone else's architecture.

Against this huge loss the shanties expressed fun, colour and improvisation, and however flimsy, they deeply belonged to those amateur architects who made them.

Late nineteenth-century legislation attacked aristocratic land-owning privilege and demanded a redistribution of land culminating in Lloyd George's 1908 budget. This led to a quarter of England changing hands in the period 1918 to 1922. Much of this land was bought by speculators, and some of the worst of it sold off as tiny building plots, which could be bought or rented cheaply. These became the 'plotlands' of the shanty explosion. Much of this was poor low-lying land, often subject to flooding. In the floods of 1953, two of the largest East Coast shanty settlements suffered worst: Jaywick suffered 35 dead and on Canvey Island 58 died.

Poorer people the world over are subject to natural disasters exactly because they are forced to live on cheap land which is vulnerable to catastrophe.

The speculators did not generally have any cultural interest in the shanty development beyond swift profits. In their hasty division of the land, they would provide simplistic grid layouts and no services. Many of the plotlands, as they were known, then became vulnerable to various attacks by authorities through the implementation of the new Public Health Acts. The planning and layout of shanty developments does not therefore represent an example of working-class culture which I would claim is evidenced in many of the actual structures.

It is worth noting that in the memories of the shanty dwellers themselves there are recorded many instances of how the move out of the smoky cities to these settlements, often by the sea with its healthier air and with fresh food from nearby farms, had distinct health advantages.

Between 1914 and 1939 the proportion of owner occupied houses had grown from 10% to 31% of all dwellings. This was supported by the growth of the mortgage companies. By this means, the landowning class sold that which they had stolen back to the people and made sure that they paid through the nose for it.

We never had a mortgage for any of them. I feel so sorry for young couples these days. They don't get the kind of chance we had. Mrs Granger, whose first plotland house was started with a borrowed pound, quoted by Hardy & Ward (1984)271 Most of the shanty builders would not have qualified for mortgages in the Twenties and Thirties. People on low wages nowadays don't have this option for housing themselves. Home ownership has become a key issue that divides the working-class:

> The growth of home ownership amongst the working-class, for example had made it harder to distinguish between people and classes on these lines although luxurious houses were certainly owned by the upper class. Devine (1992)243

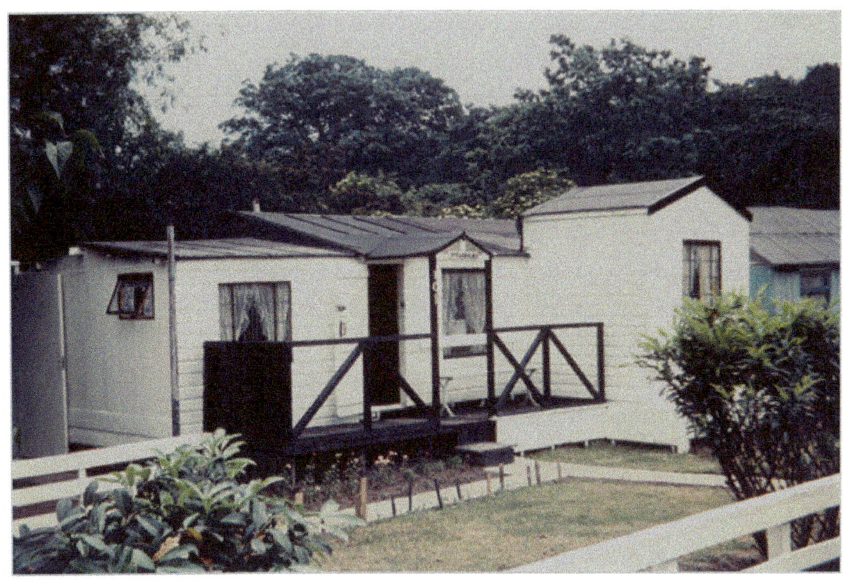

Chalet at Ovingham 1972

> The 1991 census published on 18.12.92 shows that; 'Two out of three people own their own home, a rise of 10.6 % on 1981. In contrast, just 21% live in council housing - a 9.7% fall over the past decade. The proportion of home-owners ranged from just over seven out of ten in the Southwest to just over half in Scotland.' The Independent Newspaper 19.12.92

Has the mortgage system provided the same quality of experience in housing provision? There is of course tremendous satisfaction to be gained from the process of construction. If it is the very house you are going to live in then this pleasure is magnified. However, there are other positive qualities to the experience which are not so functional. Building a house entails a large amount of collective activity, in the learning of building skills and the collection of materials, which would all be an integral part of social interaction and community formation.

It was an important realisation for me on looking closely at the shanties that still survive, and there are many of them, that people had of course been making aesthetic decisions whilst making these houses. Every detail was available for consideration and creative intervention.

Satisfaction could be gained from every successful design built and lived in. From an art and design point of view there can be little to give such deep satisfaction as the creation of your own shelter and the embellishment of this into a home. Along with clothing, water and food it is simply the most basic of human needs.

The land speculators who managed the plotlands were not always just after a fast buck; Frank Stedman, who bought the Jaywick site in 1928, was remembered by his daughter as 'a Fabian, with a sense of humour, a talented watercolour artist. People say he was on the make, but in fact he had a very strong philanthropic streak.' Like Charles Neville, who developed Peacehaven, he took an active, if paternalist, part in the development of the place throughout his active life.

It is noteworthy that at least one prominent Labour politician had a close connection with the shanty developments. George Lansbury, from Poplar, was leader of the Labour Party in 1934 and had close connections with Jaywick. He declared, 'I just long to see a start made on this job of reclaiming, recreating rural England,' so the interest of the residents wasn't entirely unrepresented in the political sphere. It was just that the shanty phenomenon wasn't seen as a significant issue. Not so surprising when we think that working-class culture was also not considered as significant, even by socialist parties. If we remember the programme that Cecil Sharp was able to inaugurate through schools with little or no adult resistance, and the fact that working-class cultural history was not a subject of serious study in those days, you get some idea of what the movement was up against.

Repression

Opposition to this self-build trend was led by a body of parliamentary socialists. Other organisations in the forefront of opposition were voluntary groups like the National Trust and Council for the Preservation of Rural England, CPRE. Support also came from voluntary bodies who also wished to 'preserve the countryside'. The overt aims of such organisations as William Morris's Society for the Protection of Ancient Buildings (or the Pure Rivers Society, or campaigns against unsightly advertising) were apparently 'rational' and could easily win widespread agreement from the electorate. However, we can now see how these elite-led organisations, operating within the unstated boundaries of good taste, were used to repress working-class culture. Often with a complete lack of understanding about what was going on.

> Since the war innumerable wooden shanties have sprung up - better sociologically but artistically deplorable. Many of these are on wheels (although unmoved for years) in order to avoid rates; and whole fields have become so packed with them that they are extremely unsanitary ... the preserver of rural amenities cannot allow any sort of old junk cabin to deform the choicest spots. Abercrombie, (1926)

This quote shows the clash of values and lack of understanding from above. The shanty builders were lumped in with the property speculators as sharing the same short-sighted commercial values. Nobody really investigated who the shanty builders were. Without doubt the shanty builders did have quite different values to the speculators; values connected with everyday living rather than making a profit or for that matter romantic concepts of landscape. For middle-class people the over-riding issue was that some crucial territories were being invaded.

> The upper classes have 'an obsessive fear of numbers, of undifferentiated hordes indifferent to difference and constantly threatening to submerge the private spaces of bourgeois exclusiveness.' Bourdieu, 1979, p.469

In spite of the forces ranged against them the shanty owners put their proletarian background to good use; often resisting local authorities' efforts to evict them.

> I wish to register my protest against the County Council's claim to have a royal prerogative over our livelihood, our destiny and our social life... The town planner dreams his way through life. There is no realism anywhere. I met town planners 40 years ago. They took a holiday in Germany and came home fanatics... the fantasy of the playboy town planner is no good to us. An anonymous voice from Shoreham Beach, quoted in an enquiry on Shoreham Beach in 1949, Hardy & Ward (1984)

The organisation and fighting spirit of places such as Jaywick was almost legendary. The charges to join the Residents Association was expensive (costing £40 per year for full time residents in 1932) but included a variety of services including street lighting and a nightly patrol of two women with dogs.

The legislation that could have made all the difference for shanty building was the Holidays-With-Pay Act of 1938, which gave nearly 11 million people holiday pay for the first time. This was the boost that the shanty movement needed and it brought the whole class conflict to a head:

> All is changed today in the English (and most of the Welsh and Scottish) sea-villages. As the politicians say, the 'danger of proletarianism is near.' Nothing but a dictatorship will save the English coast in our time ... when the millennium arrives, when battleships are turned into floating world-cruising universities, perhaps their guns, as a last act before being spiked, will be allowed to blow to dust the hideous, continuous and disfiguring chain of hotels, houses and huts which by then will have completely encircled these islands. R.M. Lockley, in Williams-Ellis (1938)

The Second World War gave the authorities an opportunity to destroy many of the coastal plotland houses as part of the Home Army's 'defence strategies'. After the war, the shanty phenomena was finally killed off as a growing cultural movement by the comprehensive Town & Country Planning Act of 1947.

Although the movement was halted as a large-scale provision of working-class housing, the incremental process of improvement and enlargement, to accommodate changing needs in the existing houses, has resulted in many thousands of desirable properties. In the same time-period many Sixties council high rises have failed and been demolished, whilst thousands of mortgaged houses have been repossessed.

Given the right supports and time to evolve, shanties could have provided mass-scale housing to high standards. I would claim that they went beyond simply meeting the need for shelter: the process of self-build, improvisational design and adventure that was involved deeply changed the people involved.

There is still quite a bit of self-build happening in Britain. In 1990, 20,000 people built their own home, a 9% increase on the previous year whilst the general figure for all newly built houses had dropped by 32% (*The Self-Builder*, spring 1991). Unfortunately, the builders are forced to imitate the utilitarian styles and building norms of the mortgage-born speculative development, so they tend to be invisible.

The shanty communities that had the potential for evolving on an urban scale were repressed more forcefully. Basildon is said to have been, 'built on heartbreak'. The heartbreak of those who lost their plotland homes in the municipal redevelopment of this new town. There is little that can now be seen of its plotland origins except for a museum with a very tidy uncreative example preserved.

Since the 1947 Act effectively disallowed spontaneous self-build, people have had to find new ways to create effective low-cost shelter that can express their own being. The inheritors of the plotland outlaw tradition in 1993, when I first wrote this, seemed to be the New Age Travelers with their impressive and sometimes intimidating convoys. As I wrote the first edition the State was preparing draconian new legislation to make this alternative lifestyle illegal. Instead of facilitating the maturing of this new culture and giving it the resources to flourish we were again in the situation in which commoners' culture was violently repressed by the state.

Housing shortage? Capital opportunity

The communities formed by the process of shanty development were usually limited in the impact they had on society by being literally outside it. If the shanties had happened within industrial towns, communities with an economic base in proletarian employment might have provided a different result. As it was, most of the plotlands tended to try to survive by being quiet and invisible; and so hope to avoid undue attention from the Local Authorities.

Various theorists of housing, like N.J. Habraken, have been

asking for the inclusion of human agency as part of the housing brief. They have inquired into what the individual can contribute to the housing process. However, until the effects of class oppression on culture are understood, such wishes will never reach fruition.

The endemic world housing-shortage can only be solved if the inherent building productivity of ordinary people is allowed to take the initiative. Not an initiative guided by the good taste of professionals but an autonomous space in which a modern urban vernacular can make mistakes, fail, learn and gradually evolve. Urban people are capable of a vernacular equal to the beauty of Devon cob cottages or any of the glories of the vernacular past eulogised by middle-class aesthetes, but the initial result might look more like a Spanish hacienda! Blueprints and utopias can only hinder us. We can only find out through a living praxis. People, given peaceful space for cultural development, will in time only surround themselves with beautiful buildings. It is only profound classism that makes anyone fear otherwise.

> An African villager looking for the first time in his life at a European House does not suspect the travail and anguish that go into building it - the ritual of buying the land with the help or hindrance of agents, lawyers and local authorities; securing a bank loan or mortgage; preparing plans, estimates, and documents indispensable for the construction of the house; and paying taxes and insurance policies on it forever after. To him the result may look elementary. Similarly, a Westerner inspecting an indigenous African dwelling may find it, too, quite plain. For what he perceives is the tangible substance, endearing in its unpretentiousness, while the all-pervading magic escapes him. He may see it as the container of a life of extreme artlessness - or what strikes him as artlessness - and may envy the owner his freedom to build, untroubled by the chicanes of bureaucracy.
> Rudofsky (1977)

Having set the scene, I now want to examine how one of the protagonists in the repression of the shanties functioned, to continue to search for the actual mechanics of oppression in an individual's action.

Clough Williams-Ellis: His early years

Williams-Ellis was born into the lower aristocracy in Wales, in 1883. His mother Ellen, an artist, had attended Ruskin's lectures and was a friend of Ralph Waldo Emerson. Clearly, she was imbued with all the current romantic ideas of rusticity and the picturesque.

> It was my mother, too, as a second stage of my keying down of the picturesque, who revealed to me the almost 'natural' beauty of the old Welsh cottages that she was so fond of sketching. To begin with, I could not allow that they had any merit or interest at all. How could a mere hovel of only two rooms with no upstairs, no stone-mullioned windows, no arched doorways even, be called beautiful or even interesting?
>
> She would not debate the question, but would quietly and very deftly make another picture. By degrees these sketches began to interest me, and I came to think them beautiful. It was not long before the attributes of interest and beauty that my mother had somehow contrived to make manifest in her pictures attached themselves to the originals, and I was soon protesting that she should not waste her time sketching animals and children when she might be so much more profitably employed in bringing out the faint yet subtle architectural flavour of the traditional 'folk-building' of our still primitive countryside.
>
> For that matter, I would do it myself - to set her a good example - she must therefore instantly teach me just exactly how one made one of these engaging and revealing pictures. I can still remember the first architectural line drawing lesson and the rapture with which I repeated again and again my mother's ingeniously simple formula for drawing a cottage. Williams-Ellis (1971)

After reading this quote it occurred to me that this apparently innocent anecdote from his childhood, the process by which a context of poverty and exploitation can be turned into a picturesque scene, could be a rare clue to the violence that must accompany the conditioning of class attitudes. It is this process by which he was anaesthetised to the social context of building design. His much trusted and beloved mother's ability repeatedly to sketch the hovel in silence, without any expression of indignation or outrage at the housing conditions of the rural poor, was a display of aloofness that could not fail to mark any young child with its symbolic absence of insight or empathy. Far from being 'revealing' the process of sketching was, I would suggest, the opposite.

The reality was different, as Richard Heath reports in *The English Peasant* (1893): 'Picturesque and harmonious from the artist's point of view, these cottages are in most respects a scandal to England.' From Peter Hall's film *Akenfield* (1970) we hear from a farm labourer: 'They wore us out without a thought' and how 'village people in Suffolk, in my day, were worked to death.' Their homes are described as hovels, sometimes little better than chicken houses!

It is within a mass of apparently innocent ordinary gestures and blanks that the culture of oppression is passed on. Later Ellis confirms the power of this process when he says: 'I shared my mother's dynastic views and regarded everything ancestoral with a reverence almost superstitious, if not indeed religious.' Williams-Ellis (1971)

This was not just a quirk of Clough's mother. It was the approach of many popular painters of the time. Acres of canvas were covered in idyllic scenes by painters such as Carlton Alfred Smith and Birkett Foster. They are still popular, fetching high prices at auction rooms around the globe. A few painters like Hubert von Herkner, who opposed the idyll with brutal realism, quickly gained notoriety. The public wanted to see poverty looking not awful, but 'authentic' and sublimely picturesque.

The picturesque is meant to illustrate the rural poor in their natural place and setting. Although they were regarded as a lower form of life, they were also supposed to have a 'dignity' within their natural state akin to the beauty of other fauna. This pseudo-respect is not extended to those varieties of this lower type of humanity who live in towns. Here they turn from picturesque peasants to a dangerous rabble or mob.

An Architect Errant

Later Clough Williams-Ellis became an architect and most of his contacts and clients, and the upper-class circles in which he moved, were inevitably conservative. However, after the First World War, he was influenced by his wife Amabel to react with a sharp swing leftwards. Amabel had herself reacted against her father who owned *The Spectator*. Her brother John Strachey was to make his mark with *The Left Book Club*, as an MP and later as a minister. Clough joined the Independent Labour Party and lectured on Town & Country Planning at their summer camp at Lady Warwick's Eastern Lodge: 'All the left wing top brass were there: Ramsay McDonald, James Maxton, Clifford Allen, Oswald and Cynthia Mosley, HG Wells.' Williams-Ellis (1971) (Oswald Mosley went on to create the British Union of Fascists in 1932.)

It seems like Socialism really gave the old owning class a chance to assert its authoritarian values in the face of the gung-ho and short-sighted capitalists that they despised. The kind of laissez faire, which suited free market values, clashed with the dynastic structure of the older gentry. This was the basis of an ongoing tension within the ruling class. As Lady Cynthia Mosley said in the House of Commons in 1930: 'The time has come when we must definitely choose between the end of 'laissez faire' or the end of rural England.'

The upper-class infiltration of the labour movement often seems to have been a tactic of counter bourgeois revolution. At the same time if they took charge of socialism they could steer the working-class well away from any serious class war and be able to moderate the excesses of the free market. In this respect, a visit to post-revolutionary Russia by Clough and other Socialists proved reassuring. At the end of the day maybe the name of the party didn't matter, as long as they got their foot in the door of power.

> From our point of view, England enjoyed almost perfect health until the beginning of the last century, when sporadic signs of a disfiguring malady began to show themselves here and there in the busier and more populous parts of our land. Williams-Ellis (1928)24

'Our' meant the owning class because the country population at the time was almost entirely poor and to his eye did not constitute a disfiguring

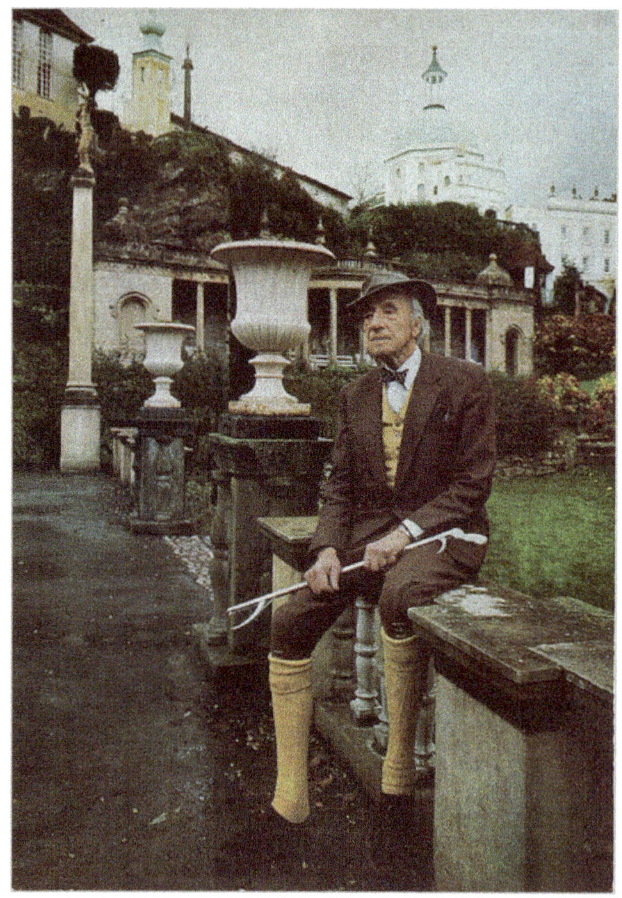

Clough Williams-Ellis 1883-1978 from the James Gardiner Collection

malady. As we have seen the rural poor was integrated into his sense of beauty through the picturesque. There was little outward evidence given of the industries that they pursued. Only with capitalism was the ugliness of exploitation externalised and expressed in depictions of the landscape. It was this despoilation of their landscape that pained the aristocracy. However, the ugliness of industry, with its pollution and blatant disregard for the earth, and the ribbon development of speculative builders, was confused with the expression of a new urban vernacular - the Plotlands.

For - need it be said? - it is chiefly the spate of mean building all

> over the country that is shriveling up the old England - mean and perky little houses that surely none but mean and perky little souls could inhabit with satisfaction ... Cultivated people of all classes must deplore what is happening. Williams-Ellis (1928)

We see here the liberal invitation to the uncouth to become cultured. There are two types of working-class people: those who take on the values of the dominant culture and so become 'cultivated', and those that do not, staying vulgar, 'mean and perky' and insensitive to beauty. This was a 'classlessness' based on the rejection of working-class culture, the precursor of our 'classless' society. 'False values, and insensitiveness - particularly to beauty - they are probably at the root of the trouble.' Williams-Ellis (1928)

In common with William Morris there was a reaction against imported taste such as the classical revival that had been brought into Renaissance England.

> It 'was no longer a customary art growing up from the bottom and out of the hearts of the people. It was a 'taste' imposed on the top as part of a subtle scheme for the dividing of gentility from servility. In England, Italian art (so-called) became a badge of the superiority of travelled people, especially those of the 'grand tour', over the people at home. It was an architecture of aristocracy provided by trained middle men of 'taste', who now wedged themselves in between the work and the workers, who were consequently beaten down to the status of mere executioners of patterns provided by a hierarchy of architectural priests.' Lethaby (1935)

These upper-class socialists did want change, something whose surface language and facade apparently related to the people, but whose deeper values were still controlled by those in high places. As we have seen this is a fundamental tactic of modern nationalism. On the foundations laid out by Ruskin, Morris and their contemporaries, good taste as an instrument of oppression, was refined by Sharp and Williams-Ellis.

Clough Williams-Ellis became something of an expert on vernacular house forms. He co-wrote a very useful book on building construction using earth and mud. This was first published as *Cottage Building in Cob, Pise, Chalk & Clay* in 1919. A later edition of it became an important source for my own first book, *Survival Scrapbook, Shelter,* which was published in 1972.

Although this interest in the vernacular fits in with an interest in socialism, it becomes apparent that he never discusses the social and economic conditions on which the form of the delightful cob cottage depended. He is blank when it comes to any real connection to knowledge about working-class life. He cannot ask obvious questions like, how did it fit into their yearly work schedule? How did they find the time and materials? How did they learn and pass on the skills required? How was social consensus on style and place achieved? What in other words were the precise social and cultural conditions that made these widely admired forms possible? The answers to these questions would have connected forward historically, and might have made it possible for people in positions of power to understand the initiatives the new urban populations were taking to develop their own vernacular forms.

The same sorts of questions were asked neither by Sharp and the song collectors, nor by William Morris and his associates. The point that I cannot over-emphasize is that this was not simply an oversight by enthusiasts; nor was it the result of 'evil' men. They were simply incapable of asking these questions, of obtaining this knowledge, because of their class conditioning.

Town Planning

In the first half of the twentieth century there arose the new profession of Town Planning. The town planners knew nothing of working-class life, culture or community. The information that they had on their clients was a projection of their own fantasies and stereotypes, and bore only the faintest resemblance to reality. Someone like Williams-Ellis could wallow in this ignorance and yet present his lack of information with such panache that it seemed part of being the consummate professional.

By making his pronouncements from a socialist platform, the illusion of being on the side of the people was complete. When talking of the redevelopment of towns he wrote vaguely of the requirement for 'heroic measures' and 'large loans'; a park would apparently replace the slums. There was no mention of what would happen to the slum dwellers and their relation to the required heroism and large loans! He also seemed incredibly naive in how these suggestions could be used by those commercial forces he professed to hate. As was proven with acute force in the Sixties, large-scale redevelopment was the place where really huge profits could be creamed off - it didn't really matter if the place stayed empty or even if it got pulled down later; the money was to be made in the process of development.

His rhetoric was however, emotionally appealing to the lower classes, because he used his literary fluency to attack their common enemy. As I have pointed out, his classism was invisible. A large body of public opinion could therefore be found to support his position.

Reasonably he attacked the speculators: 'Each of these parceled out his own [land] purchase into little building plots in his own quite futile fashion; with no attempt at co-ordination or a general idea.' Williams-Ellis (1928)

He left out an important consideration; this was the only chance for many lower-class people to get control of a plot of land and build their own house; and he did not make any differentiation between these two groups in his attack. Peacehaven, a south coast seaside town, was the classic example of this 'distressing and almost universal complaint.' It was with 'their gratuitously flashy or exotic appearance that fault is found. Laid out with sense and designed with sensibility, a seaside Bungalow Town might be charming.' Williams-Ellis (1928)142

Peacehaven was singled out for particularly vicious criticism because, apart from its siting on the South Downs, it was urban in scale and potential.

> Unless you wish to see how ugly a thing man can make of beauty, avoid the cliffs between Newhaven and Brighton... The poison begins at Peacehaven, which until thirteen or fourteen years ago was a piece of unspoilt downland open to the sea. It is now a colony of shacks, a long ungainly street of houses that all seem ashamed of themselves. Mais (1938)

> A monstrous blot on the national conscience. Howard Marshal in Williams-Ellis (1938)

It may have been different if he or his class could have designed and planned the bungalows, but otherwise he hated the tasteless results of working-class creativity as much as he hated the thoughtlessness and myopia of the speculator:

> The adventurous bungalow plants its foundations - a pink asbestos roof screaming its challenge across a whole parish from some pleasant upland that it has lightheartedly defaced. Williams-Ellis (1929)

> Good architecture is not necessarily conspicuous, and never pretentious: order is the first essential. Williams-Ellis & Summerson (1934)6

Order seemed to require a synthesis; which required the overview of town planners; which, in turn, required the strong central authority of the state. We can see how the shanties would have clashed with every aspect of his sense of governance and good taste. Even within a profession, this authoritarian command structure is enacted.

> New architectural ideas filter down from the top, and the lesser architects imitate what the great men in the profession are doing. Williams-Ellis & Summerson (1934)10

However, in retrospect he did sympathise with the shanty builders on one thing, on which he imagines that he and they agree:

> It was easy to do nothing but revile those who thus spoiled the country with nauseous little buildings, or merely to laugh darkly at their tragic failure to achieve an imagined rusticity. But it was unjust, cynical and lazy - like cursing a stricken family because in escaping from its burning home it trespassed over lawns and flower beds. Williams-Ellis (1951)

I wonder if people were fleeing urbanisation? There was not the opportunity to self-build within towns - if there had been, a different story would almost certainly have emerged.

Clough was a foremost supporter of Garden Cities and chaired the committee responsible for Stevenage New Town. In *Around the World In 90 Days* (1978), he said: 'We have, first, to be thinking all the time about living human beings.' We realise the absurdity of this only when he goes on to describe the sensation caused amongst the new town planners at the end of the Fifties with the arrival of Wilmot & Young's ground-breaking study *Family and Kinship in the East London.* This was notable as one of the first modern sociological surveys of working-class life and it exploded many stereotypical assumptions that planners had relied upon. The people in Wilmot & Young's survey were not organised into neat little nuclear families but belonged to extended kinship groups with all kinds of patterns of complex community completely unsuspected by the planners.

In spite of this report they didn't seem able or willing effectively to change their approach and modify their subsequent developments to respond to such objective data. Their blankness was more entrenched than a simple lack of information.

The Sham of Public Consultation

It must be said that Ellis did attempt some consultative procedures, but they were so laden with class prejudice and ignorance that they were doomed to failure. In a little untitled chapbook written for the Industrial Discussion Clubs Experiment (IDCE), published in the 1940s to advise workers on their responsibilities, Ellis begins candidly:

> No one else can quite do this sort of thinking for you, because no-one else knows just how you live, or would like to live.' He appeals for workers; 'to say what it is you, the customer, require,' because if you do not do this 'loudly and insistently' then, 'it will scarcely be the planners, fault if they dish up something you don't want at all.' Williams-Ellis (1940s) unpublished paper.

He is not only expecting us to be able to translate spatial desires into language, but to be able to put them into a literary form that his class and profession can understand; in other words, to be able to speak their language. And if you do not manage all this in your spare time, if you have any, then it will not be the planners' fault if you have to live in a concrete shit-hole the rest of your life. This is not the only pitfall of this exercise in 'planning democracy'. Continuing to quote from the same chapbook:

'Quite often money could actually be saved by leaving out such silly trimmings as sham half timbering and quite meaningless whim-whams that only fuss a building up and make it look a fool.' Here we are aware that only certain types of suggestions would be acceptable anyway! The things that working-class people tend to do to their houses are poo-pooed as silly, meaningless, foolish and in poor taste, so a further difficulty here is that all the suggestions must not only be in middle-class cultural terms but also be quite congruent with middle-class aesthetic values.

'Forget about fashion and what the Joneses might want you to have,' he goes on in the same chapbook. People are exhorted to leave the whole basis of the social and communicative processes of cultural consensus formation and to strike out into a brave new individualist world of accepting guidance on good taste and modernity from above.

Throughout the IDCE chapbook there is an assumption of the profound correctness of his position and the myth that rational thought would lead everyone to the same conclusions. At the same time, his arrogance is cut by an absurdly fey expression of doubt, 'The fact is, we architects and town planners are a bit in the dark about what people want, yet there are tens of thousands of people in your district alone for whom we are going to be asked to build'.

He also warns us: 'You are unlikely to get everything you want'; with some guidance as to the realistic limitations to be faced: 'Would you like to save a shilling a week in rent by reducing room heights (from 8') to 7' 6" or even 7'?' In several more outrageous questions like these he reminds the workers how they can get more money in their pocket for booze and fags if they agree to live like rats. They are constantly reminded that the quality of their conditions is dependent on their ability to pay, ignoring both the productive capacity of working-class skills to transcend this limitation and the fact that shelter is a basic need and a human right. He ends this 'generous and progressive' outreach:

Post on a copy of your report to the secretary, the Housing Centre, Suffolk St., Pall Mall, London SW1, who will see that your opinions are compared with those from other districts and brought to the notice of the 'high ups.'

In this extraordinary conclusion, we are infantalised whilst being reminded of those high above us who 'inevitably' and mysteriously run our lives. The Pall Mall address lends it the air of a royal court. There is no offer to publish the reports or pass copies around the senders. In other words, the eternal power of the 'high ups', with its connotation of the working-class as children, is sealed.

The results of this kind of classist stupidity resulted in the largest scale of violence to working-class people this century, barring only the world wars. Beautiful urban community structures and culture, built-up over several generations, were decimated by the mass break-up and relocation of hundreds of thousands of people through the Fifties and Sixties. The people were often moved out to New towns or dispersed in housing in which it was difficult to remake these connections, in which an indoor toilet, hot water taps and central heating were exchanged for alienation. Large parts of Southwark, which I overlooked when I first wrote this, were covered with massive concrete high-rise blocks, which have invariably generated profound environmental and social problems when used as family housing.

William Morris was not immune from this vision of tall blocks of flats 'in what might be called vertical streets' May Morris II, quoted by Thompson (1955)129. It was thought high-rise housing would free the land from squalid workers' dwellings and create healthy parkland. One of Morris's favourite derogatory words was 'makeshift'. This is a word consciously applied to the shanties by Hardy and Ward in the subtitle of their book.

Spatial Deconcentration

On a smaller scale, even council house allocation programmes have perpetuated this dislocation and disruption of community. All this is a crime the enormity of which has yet to be assessed because classism doesn't allow us to see it. Somehow it got passed off as the normal path of progress or even a proud socialist housing 'provision'. Although recent social housing design is improving, with low-rise housing as the norm, there is now little money.

At the time that the shanty phenomena was happening the propaganda of modern architecture was being loudly trumpeted and must have drowned out any working-class thought of protest. I have not come across any radical study that reveals a strategy of breaking-up working-class community in London, or elsewhere in Britain, but it has become an unspoken establishment tradition. Here is a description of the same sort of strategy in operation in the USA published by the Yulanda Ward Memorial Fund in 1980 and reprinted in *No Reservations, Housing, Space and Class Struggle,* in 1991:

> It was not until 1979 that we discovered and began to research a federal government programme called Spatial Deconcentration, the hidden agenda behind the phenomenon of displacement. We discovered that displacement had an economic base to be sure, but more importantly, it was a means of social control - a means to break up large concentrations of Blacks and other inner-city minorities from their communities. We have witnessed the forced evacuation of more than 50,000 poor inner city residents from the city each year and their subsequent replacement by an affluent class. We understood the role of the government and its officials as it aided this process by creating laws that benefited landlords and speculators while impoverishing tenants, but it wasn't until Department of Housing and Urban Development (HUD) documents began to surface using the words 'housing mobility' and 'fair housing' that we began to understand the magnitude of the masterplan to rid the city of its inner-city poor and working-classes. To fully understand this programme we had to understand its history, the atmosphere out of which it developed, and its objectives. After this we had concrete answers to why 50,000 poor people a year are being driven into Prince George's, Montgomery, Prince William, and other suburban jurisdictions increasingly further away from the inner city, while central city neighbourhoods are allowed to decay until speculators and middle-class whites move in to take them over. Ward (1980)

This federal government programme called Spatial Deconcentration, which came out of recommendations made by the Kerner Commision, began in 1969 and received investments of over five billion dollars. This principle of urban land value has been repeated globally.

If home is where the heart is, then it was the destruction of the shanty initiative by the 1947 Town and Country Planning Act, followed by the mass housing profiteering of the Fifties, Sixties and Seventies, which destroyed the heart of many existing or nascent working-class communities, through programmes of community fragmentation and spatial deconcentration.

What the dominant culture always fears most is the mob - a big crowd in an ebullient mood. It is just at such times when the deadening weight of powerlessness can be thrown off and an insight gained into our true collective power. In a large gathering of people information can spread quickly without state mediation. In the short term this holds the threat of riot; but in England at least, spontaneous riot is a recognised way of putting state measures of relief in motion. A traditional part of British culture in which the classes negotiate their consensus through deed and the oppressed let off steam, (see Thompson (1991). The crowd which meets repeatedly is more deeply worrying. This unease underlies the state repression of raves with their hi-tech M25 mobile phone communication networks and the revival (c1993) of the circuit of alternative fairs and festivals, as well as the 'spatial deconcentration' of inner-city poor.

Prisoners of Good Taste

How can such benign bureaucrats as Williams-Ellis be responsible for crimes of such magnitude - these eloquent men with their elegance, glamour and charisma? Their pompous posture of inane self-assurance was a masquerade behind which was nothing but a massive blank classist stupidity. Typically the opposite of their victims in whom intelligence is masked by a lack of self-confidence.

To me this blankness is reified in the twentieth century townscape. Everywhere you find blanks, gaps and spaces which don't make sense, that have just been left without meaning or function, surfaces which sit there staring out with nothing to say, nothing to reflect. People fill these blanks with litter and graffiti – is this an inchoate protest? Even the official idealistic public open spaces have become too expensive to maintain. Gradually they become derelict, an anti-monument to municipal socialism's abstract 'citizen'.

Clough Williams-Ellis is most famous for designing Portmeirion, a fantasy village built in North Wales in the fifties where many European vernaculars are collaged together in a celebration of the picturesque. All white, and weirdly alienating as only a village which imitates an organic real village could be - nearby at Transfynydd is a Magnox nuclear reactor which stands on common land, that was compulsorily bought by the War Office in 1905.

> Lewis Mumford contrasted the Mega-machine at Transfynydd with the charm of neighbouring Portmeirion... but may they not be two sides of the same coin? Reed (1991)30

It has become world famous as the film-set for Patrick McGoohan's unsettling TV series of the Sixties, *The Prisoner*. In this programme The Prisoner, played by McGoohan, repeatedly attempts to escape from neatly-dressed figures and mysterious forces of oppression. He is constantly interrogated and threatened but refuses to give up his own judgement, his autonomy. The terror and coercion behind the facade of sixties' normality is revealed.

Clough had clearly designed Portmeirion as his answer to 'those mean and perky shacks', but one mastermind attempting to design the indeterminacy of an organically evolved village can only produce a crude imitation of the subtle complexity produced by incremental communitarian development:

> In the biological world, there is always an immense complexity: and this complexity comes about as the result of a process of minute adaptations, which painstakingly, slowly, ensures that every part is properly adapted to its conditions. Christopher Alexander, quoted by Reed (1991)37

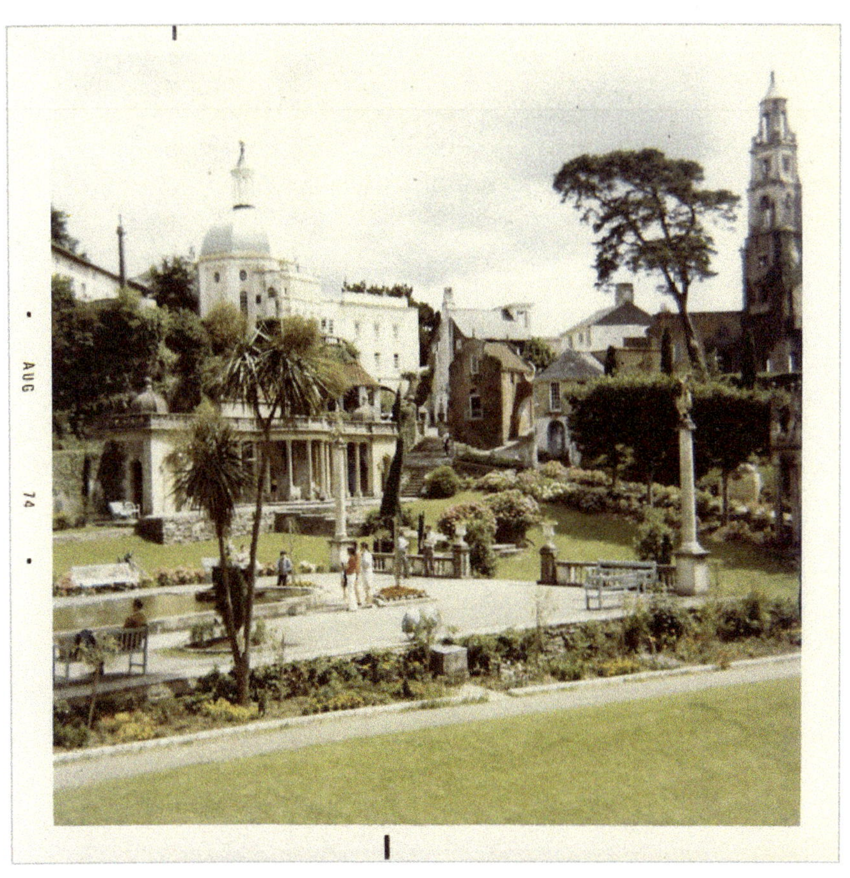

Photograph of Portmeirion by SteveR 1974

The city streets had such rich potential for meeting, but the garden cities and suburbs successfully diverted people's desire for togetherness to material possessions and cut people off from one another. The potential of the crowd was diluted. The Prisoner had no name - he was called only 'Number 6': He protests: "I am not a number! I am a free man!" He was imprisoned in The Village and although The Village had no walls he could not escape. It looked picturesque and pleasant, but behind the scenes people are tortured and killed if they did not 'give the right answers'. Most of The Village's inhabitants led a bland zombie like existence doing exactly what was suggested in spite of a charade of democracy. What the rulers were really after was forever a mystery. Did they even know themselves? Were we all complicit? The director of The

Village, known as No 2, gave speeches praising 'social responsibility' and 'participation' but these were empty platitudes. Everyone had 'rights' but there was no real freedom to have your own thoughts and values. Language had lost its meaning: 'Of the people, by the people, for the people,' the emptiness of these socialist slogans echoed around Ellis' monument.

McGoohan was, unusually, given a free hand in the making of The Prisoner, after his highly successful commercial series Danger Man. It was very weird and experimental when it was shown in the Sixties and became a cult classic after it was repeated in the Seventies. It revealed, as only such a freely-made cinematic drama can, the violent alienation that results when a people's culture is replaced by a disinfected reconstruction of itself. We are all similarly imprisoned and disenfranchised by the invisible and undefinable 'je ne sais quoi' of Good Taste.

A Short History of Oppression

Exploitation has always been dependent on oppression. Exploitation is the process by which people are paid less for their work than the value of what they produce. On top of that they have no say in what they produce. The surplus value of what they produce is creamed off by the owning-class. What is produced is decided by what produces the most profit. This is a description of capitalism as thoroughly analysed by Karl Marx. Driven by greed for short-term profits it is immensely destructive and violent, but also productive - showering the planet with glittering commodities. Some of these are very useful; some are weapons; some are wondrous gadgets; some diversionary games and some are addictive drugs.

The owners control their system of exploitation and protect their own class and its vast accumulated wealth, by means of 'oppression'. By oppression I mean the institutionalised mistreatment of one group by another.

Because the owning-class are richer and more powerful than the rest of us they have persuaded themselves this must be because they are innately superior. The rest of us are therefore to be treated as inferior. Initially using naked violence, later partially replaced with deft control of culture, media and education, this false consciousness is driven home with such force that most of us have to a greater or lesser extent internalised it. Deep down we feel we are incapable of taking power. From this point, the superiority-inferiority nexus, common to all oppression, spawns a great variety of forms.

Part of the mythology of aristocratic superiority was that it is genetic - down to good breeding. There is now a broad consensus that the main differences between human beings are newly imposed on every generation. Class differences are not simply a matter of wrong ideas, which could easily be corrected by offering better information. The only way class conditionings can be fixed, with at least the appearance of permanence, is by a more violent and somatic process of encryption, a process which entails damage to the integrity of our organism. The only way people can be persuaded that they are inferior or superior is through persistent *hurtful* conditioning, although these processes have been normalised to the degree that they seem only natural or inevitable.

If we get hurt, there are two rational courses of action. Once the danger is past and we are in a safe place, the first preferred action is for us to heal from the hurt. Emotional healing is accompanied spontaneously by physiological phenomena such as crying, shaking, laughter and lively non-repetitive talking. When emotional process subsides, and it can be quite a prolonged and social process, the next logical step is to change our world so that this does not happen again. For oppression to exist it is essential that these two processes have to be systematically inhibited.

If healing cannot occur, the hurts are retained in the memory along with the recordings of what happened at the time the hurt occurred. This storage of hurt embedded with a particular memory interferes with our functioning whenever the original memory is evoked by present time experiences. This interference takes several forms:

1. It numbs us or makes us forget.

2. It confuses our thinking or functioning (causing dis-ease).

3. It causes irrational or perverse behaviour.

So, what might humans be like without the weight of this heritage of oppression? I think they would be highly adaptive, flexibly intelligent, culturally inventive, more cooperative and much less reactive, destructive and violent. They would also have social processes and skills that allowed everyone to recover from hurts.

A relatively straightforward mundane example might be in the eating patterns of my own history. It's taken me forty years to move towards a non-rigid but more rational food intake that responds to my real present-time physical needs. Only two generations back my Granny had times in her young life when famine was a real possibility. After ten children had been born, her father died, leaving Great Granny Johnson to fend for herself with no social security. In common with many rural people, food was supplemented by such means as gleaning. I can imagine her excitement when she was sent away into service as a pastry cook. Many people at this time did not have ovens and so food was generally cooked by boiling. It must have been a real treat to eat cakes and pastries. My mother in her time made delicious pastries, cakes and puddings which had a profound appeal to me. As a child I was incessantly told to eat all my food up because the people in Africa were starving. Amazing value was placed on 'a clean plate' and a 'good appetite'. The point is that these insecurities are not very far away in many of our lives. My occupation means that I spend many hours seated in front of a computer, but often I eat much more than this activity requires. It has been the old hurts associated with food, which go back to anxiety about starvation, that have been passed on to me by a complex chain of mealtime behaviours. Patterns of hurt are handed down through generations, often in coded ways, if they are not resolved.

On a wider scale our society's addiction to sugar can be traced back to abuse on a much grander scale. Black slaves in the colonies produced cheap energy-food, with no nutritional value, for the working classes back in Britain. There are more sweet taste buds on the tongues of young people, and children are particularly vulnerable to this legacy of slavery. Our daily life is impregnated with habituated actions and attitudes which are perversions of our desires caused by oppression. When hurtful experience distorts our instinctual desires, for food, speech or sex, it is particularly deep-rooted and resistant to change.

Recovery processes are never lost, only repressed to some degree. It also seems that the majority, and perhaps all, of the accumulated hurts may be healed by these processes. Human functioning is always tending to find ways towards the expression and resolution of these buried hurts.

The Oppressor Role is a Dehumanising One

The oppressors or the dominant classes must therefore hurt other people, or actively maintain a system of hurtful conditioning, to persuade people that they are inferior. Now, it would not be possible for oppressors to inflict suffering on large numbers of people without repressing certain of their own inborn human sensibilities. An assumption I'm making here is that a human who has not been hurt would resist hurting other people. The suppression of this human instinct to care can only be achieved and maintained through violent conditioning. that must also include the suppression of healing or recovery processes. It is conditioning such as this that prepares the youth of the dominant classes for their future roles. The basic principles are the same for any dominant oppressor group, whether it is adults, men or the 'upper' classes.

For the reproduction of the upper classes the first thing is the suppression of a sympathetic emotional response towards the condition of the majority of the population. The famous 'stiff-upper-lip' is a signifier of this attitude. The superior class is characterised by its cool intellectual responses and pleasures. This emotional surgery must be carried out early in life whilst the human is vulnerable. In preparation for their future roles, ruling class young people are systematically and viciously hurt often by the simple expedient of removing them from parental care and sending them away to a boarding school.

This cool, detached, intellectual identity is then presented to the whole of society, as characteristic of superiority. It also presents as a model to which anybody who wishes to assume a higher status, become a real man, be a respectable citizen, be normal and so on must aspire. These are the first universal principles of all oppressor conditioning. A young man who expresses painful emotion may be told not 'to be such a woman' or 'not to be a baby.'

The second level of oppressor culture entails a withdrawal and distancing from the productive roles and lives of those in the inferior class. Characteristics associated with physical work tend to be devalued. For example, dirt, especially dirty hands and dirty fingernails, are associated with the working class. Many such characteristics of working-class people become repugnant to the upper classes. On the other hand, the activities which characterise the oppressive role are given positive values; elevated posture, slow glances, restraint, lack of agitation or eagerness, even sitting still! A reserved detachment is the ideal. This adds up to a complete inability to perceive the real lives of the majority of people. The facts are replaced with myths and stereotypes that are a projection of the subjectivities of the ruling classes.

So, both oppressor and oppressed are reduced by the process. These principles, which underlie the reproduction of oppression, frame the cultural production that is possible with the excess wealth available to the oppressor through the processes of exploitation. This value stolen from the lower classes and accumulated by the upper, as well described in classic socialist theory, inevitably produces an impressive culture that is made by very skilled artists and artisans. Wealth can be used to produce what is known in Britain as excellence. Excellence is that extra skill and attention to detail, complexity and judgement that can be put into works of culture, when the artist can focus on the work full-time. The production of this excellence has been claimed as justification enough for all the evils of exploitation, but we find that this claim is made by those who do not really know the oppressed people they are talking about. This top layer of oppressor culture is often rich with 'life affirming' content which serves to camouflage and disguise the underlying oppression. This fine icing hides the rotten cake.

How does this process affect those of us that are the target for this oppression? If a person has been deeply hurt and they are denied a rational response, it seems that they tend to act out the hurt on someone else. This has recently been observed in the gradual uncovering of child abuse. Child abusers have nearly always been abused themselves. The ‘cycle of abuse’ is a widely-recognised phenomenon, which could help explain how oppression is maintained with the minimum of force. People are not only hurt by oppression but will then often look for other people who they can debase and so feel superior to, seeking, in this way, some apparent relief for their own intolerable feeling of inferiority. This self-perpetuating abuse then divides the non-owners into an endless array of further conflicting factions. We are all caught up to our necks in this mire.

Society becomes endlessly ranked with everyone feeling superior and inferior to someone else. It would be tragicomic were the results in human suffering not so hideous.

Oppression can be defined, as I have suggested, as the institutionalised and culturally integrated devaluation and systematic abuse of a particular class of people by another dominant class. In a consumer society, which has generally overcome base necessity, oppression and the misery and dis-ease it causes is still rampant, and is the most urgent thing in the way of human flourishing.

The good news is that, to an unknown degree, we can recover from most if not all of our early hurts, at any stage in our life. We still have all our power intact, although it may be temporarily occluded. It seems that if the true nature of our reality can be demonstrated with sufficient vividness the process of healing takes place spontaneously. At such times, we feel in touch with our real power.

The public places where I have most vividly experienced this contradiction of the false reality of oppression were in Portsmouth at the time of the student takeover of my college and in Brixton during the 1981 riots. The most widespread example I have witnessed shows how these things do not always happen in a politically right-on context! When the first non-Italian Pope for centuries returned home to Poland he gave the whole country what amounted to a massive pep talk. He reminded Poles of their inherent dignity and their persistent struggles against the most vicious oppressors and invaders. He reminded them that, as battered and defeated as they had been, they had survived, they were still intact, they still had their dignity, they were good people and still capable of realising their freedom. Hundreds of thousands of people broke down and cried maybe for the first time, as adults, at these 'sermons'. I know this is difficult for non-Poles to understand, as the difference between observing emotions and feeling them is critical. A few years later Solidarność appeared and I am convinced that this event, which itself contradicted Poles' second-class European status, was causal.

> The first pilgrimage by John Paul II to Poland in 1979
> considerably contributed to producing an atmosphere in which a year later Solidarity could emerge. Dialogue & Humanism (1991)

A Brief history of Good Taste 1650 - 1790

Aristocratic Taste

Baltasar Gracián was a Spanish Jesuit writer on French aristocratic courtly taste in the period immediately preceding the rise of the bourgeoisie. In his book *Oráculo manual y arte de prudencia* (1647) a collection of 300 aphorisms, he wrote of the requirement of those in court to disguise themselves and present only the appearance required by convention and the sovereign. They had to 'cultivate a happy spontaneity' and practise discretion. There were no formal rules; taste was meant to be intrinsic to a particular type of human. Taste was the 'Je ne sais quoi,' the indefinable quality of superiority, innate to those with good breeding. It was important that it was played out intuitively otherwise it would have been too wooden - yet it was still a facade of appearances generated by the power of the aristocracy. This creation of the appearance of happiness, through the coercion of those in courtly circles, was a powerful force, which on the one hand represses the expression of hurt, and on the other led to the modern expression of glamour. Even in the provincial courts of princes and feudal barons we find:

> The manner of social intercourse, the expression of emotion, indeed the emotions themselves... all these are stereotyped... within the bounds of more or less rigid conventions. Hauser (1951)189

Given the distributive power of modern media, this hell of smiley faces has been imposed on all. Rather than being a global village the world is more like a decadent bourgeois version of an aristocratic royal court. This fake happiness, which masked a terror of the almighty sovereign, was one key aspect of aristocratic culture. Another was the code of honour and its ritual resolution of conflict, dueling.

ORACVLO
MANVAL,
Y
ARTE DE PRVDENCIA.
SACADA
DE LOS AFORISMOS
QVE SE DISCVRRẼ
En las obras de
LORENÇO GRACIAN.
PVBLICALA
D. VINCENCIO
IVAN DE LASTANOSA,
I la dedica
Al Excelẽtiſsimo Señor
D. LVIS MENDEZ
DE HARO,
CONDE DVQVE.

Con licencia: Impreſſo en Hueſca, por Iuan Nogues, Año 1647.

The inhumanity that a class society requires of its rulers is not only channeled from the top down, it is a general virulent psychosis amongst the dominant class which might be directed at anyone who gets in the way. This is illustrated by the history of dueling. Although it was banned in the British army in 1844, the custom continued in Russia and Germany until the 1920s or later. During the eighteenth century in England it rivaled fox hunting as the favourite bloodsport of the upper classes.

> It was condemned by Queen Elisabeth's Privy Council some years later but to little effect, for by this time it was considered a social accomplishment and therefore subject to the usual social pressures despite being denounced as little more than 'illustrious and honourable murders' - presumably up and coming young

> blades would rather run the risk of being called murderers than be without honour ... It was this code of honour which acted like a psychological spur against so many reluctant flanks, forcing normally rational and pacific men to risk their lives for what were by modern standards often the most trivial of reasons. Loose (1983)3

Sometimes these reasons were simply minor breaches of etiquette, showing the fear and tension running below the surface of this society. On one occasion, a man hit another's dog; another time a remark was considered impertinent; both incidents resulted in fatal duels. Dr Johnson commented:

> He, then, who fights a duel, does not fight from passion against his antagonist, but out of self-defense; to avert the stigma of the world, and to prevent himself from being driven out of society. Quoted in Loose (1983)4

This shows how powerful and deep is our desire to be an acceptable part of society. It is this instinct which drives reasonable people to take part in massacres or be guards in concentration camps. It is this desire to be included, to be part of society and the corresponding fear of being outcast that can be manipulated to maintain order. The emphasis on the sublimation of passion is typical of upper class culture.

> I cannot impress upon an individual too strongly the propriety of remaining perfectly calm when hit; he must not allow himself to be alarmed or confused; but summoning up all his resolution, treat the matter coolly; and, if he dies, go off with as good grace as possible. The Art of Dueling, 1836, quoted by Loose (1983)5

> It was: The ultimate expression of the code of honour by which the upper classes lived ... The lower classes did not conduct affairs of honour, having none: they conducted brawls, fortunately for them, as Hannah More, a leading Evangelist, pointed out: 'Honour is the religion of tragedy.' Loose (1983)3

If dueling was the ritual by which the owning class resolved conflicts, then the working-class ritual of conflict resolution in parts of Britain was called 'rough music.' (See: E.P Thompson, 1991). Someone who broke social codes of morality was ritually disgraced and, in extreme cases, driven out by the action of a crowd, who visited the home of the perpetrator armed with noisy instruments and created a rumpus to publicise their misdemeanours. This could be cruel and unjust and it could be a vehicle for communal bigotry - occasionally people were physically hurt. The intention, however, was clearly the displacement of violence, the venting of anger, not upon the person of the victim, but in ritual form.

Dueling involves a sublimation of emotion whereas rough music was an attempt to discharge emotion. The great potential of working-class cultures is that they tend to incorporate more healthy expressions of emotion. This is also true of any culture of people who are oppressed e.g. women or black peoples. These practices are important as they may contain the seeds which we may be able to cultivate to recover from the legacy of oppression. These characteristics of oppressed groups are often presented as failing and things to be ashamed of rather than a potential path to liberation.

The medieval nobles had a need of a culture of war to maintain their dominance over their subjects. This violence, which was available to be unleashed on the subject population, was demonstrated and developed in warfare against other nobles and sovereign cities. For aristocrats who spurned the new bourgeois accomplishments of trade, finance and manufacture, war was the main way that wealth could be increased.

War was so central to the maintenance of the status quo that the ability to wage war had to be valued above purely hereditary claims to nobility. Skill in the art of arms was a pathway to upward mobility. Brave deeds in battle could be rewarded with land, title, plunder and, above all, honour. This potential upward mobility by virtue of arms would also serve to warn the European ruling classes against going soft and becoming vulnerable to revolution and barbarism.

Chivalry offered a set of values which regulated this noble violence. Chivalry was the code by which a noble's violence was dressed up in civilised garb. The greatest honour was held to be death or glory on the battlefield. It was essential that this was stage-managed to be witnessed by the right audience or nothing was achieved.

The culture of chivalry also included heraldry, chivalric orders, tournaments and courtly demeanour. Taken to its logical conclusion the cult of chivalry resulted in 'man as a fighting machine' with few surviving human qualities. He disliked music and dance, did not sing or hunt, and was indifferent to lovemaking, Vale (1981)163. Here was 'the knight in shining armour', the great model of manhood as perpetuated through stories such as the Arthurian Legends. The model that, as we have seen, was held in high esteem by William Morris.

The technology of firearms and the resulting depersonalisation of war during the later fifteenth century caused individual combat, a crucial source of glory for the male aristocrat, to die out. The rise of the duel in the sixteenth century seems to have been the compensation.

Thomas Hobbes was one of the earliest modern philosophers at a time when the power of the sovereign was still absolute. In his book *Leviathan,* published in 1651, he described his belief that society would be chaotic, but for the presence of the sovereign. He observed that the sovereign clearly did not order society any more by direct coercive force but by his magnetic influence as a personification of order. It was the people's belief in the image of the sovereign that united them. Hobbes theorised that order in society was dependent on the spectacle of authority that emanated from the sovereign.

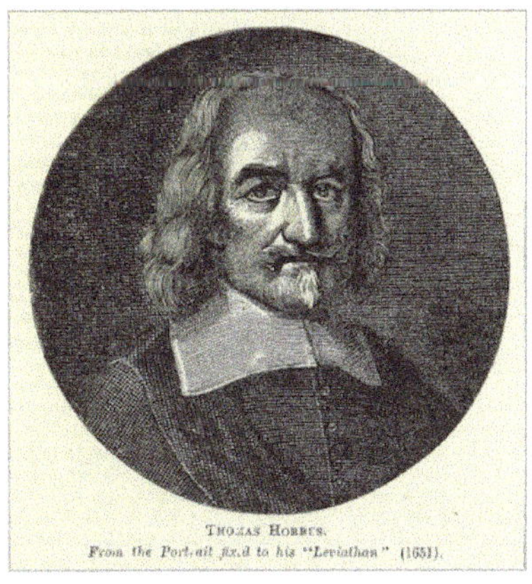

Thomas Hobbes 1588–1679

The people had come to believe in the 'divine right of kings', a belief that the sovereign was naturally superior and necessary. Once this belief was internalised there was less need for naked violence. In fact, Hobbes argued against the divine right but still supported the sovereign against parliament.

The diversity of human beings united in their belief in the sovereign was seen as similar to the operation of the imagination, which distils a single thought or image from the manifold of our sensory impressions. In this way Hobbs suggested that the political system was a natural and inevitable outcome of human functioning. The use of this analogy, as if there is a real causal connection between the nature of human physiology and political structure, became a continuing ruse in the development of bourgeois philosophy. Hobbes' 'Leviathan' revealed the fragility of the power of the sovereign ruler and the cultural forces which kept it intact.

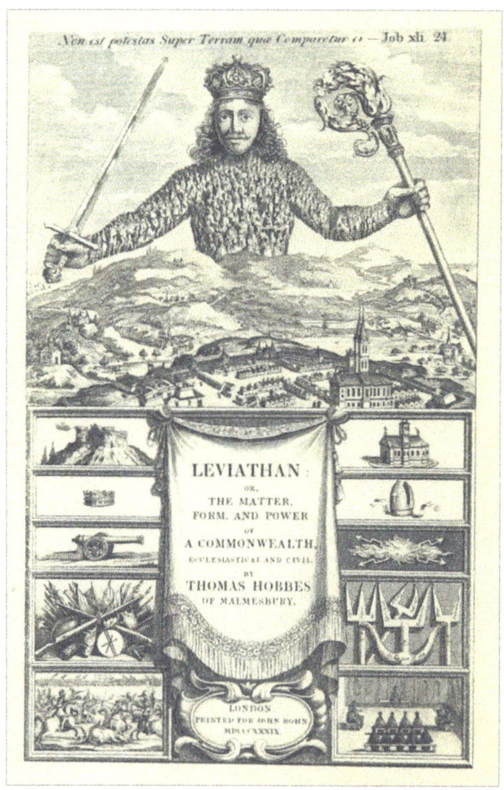

> Should their gaze turn away from the spectacle and towards each other, then the illusion of stage would be destroyed along with their unity as an audience. The unification of diversity follows from individuals in the audience producing the illusion which constitutes them as an audience. Caygill (1989)24

Bourgeois Taste

From the start of the first millennium there had been secular scribes and scholars who had worked for the more powerful aristocrats in Northern Italy. These people, who later became known as Humanists, studied writing from ancient Greece and Rome which were held up as the classics of literary culture. These people were employed to administer the early city states. Universities were formed for mutual protection and study - the first was in Bologna in 1088. This institution played an important part in studying Roman Law and adapting it for Medieval times.

As aristocratic rule reached its apogee in Europe, there was developing a new class of rich merchants, bankers and craft guilds whose interests were different to that of the aristocracy whose wealth was based on the ownership and control of land. Land ownership profoundly underlies the interests and values of aristocratic culture. The new class benefited from the activity of the humanists especially after the invention of printing with moveable type in 1450. Knowledge, codified in printed books, led to an explosion of secular discourses across Europe which became known as The Enlightenment; a period that lasted from about 1650 to 1750. The use of literary reasoning led to science and to rapid technological advances. The ensuing products were exchanged through the medium of money. Books are often considered as the first commodities. Reason, books and money became central to the outlook and culture of this new class.

The new bourgeoisie still aspired to courtly manners and country estates, although these people were on the whole less ostentatious and were more interested in social regulation through law than through the use of blood and sword.

The rational project of science was led by 'men of genius' who, by observing and measuring the natural world, discovered universally applicable laws. Applied in combination these rules led to a vast increase in productivity. Understandably some of these men applied their methods of thinking to understand human functioning, both on the individual and social level, using reason to speculate on those matters that could not be objectively measured. This thinking created modern philosophy.

In the development of bourgeois culture, philosophy became an important ritual of justification and training for intellectuals. The rational project and its progeny, science, demonstrated a vast superiority over magic and religion as a stimulus to production and as a means to achieve efficient social control. The old metaphysics was gradually overwhelmed by the new rational consciousness. The victorious mercantile and industrialist class claimed this power of reason as their birthright. It was the cause of their superiority, the key to their wealth. They stereotyped their whole class as primarily intellectual and rational beings. Just as the 'higher' faculties held the 'lower' emotions and sensualities in tight control so the higher classes controlled the lower. The people not in this higher class, who were by definition inferior, were supposed not to have this intellectual faculty. They were not yet civilised and like animals were supposed to be characterised by their sensory, emotional, sexual, instinctive and intuitive behaviour. The thing that made humans distinct from animals was their ability to reason with language. People who could not demonstrate these civilised characteristics were considered not to be fully human. The old badges of class superiority like honour and chivalry were overtaken by an abstract and detached intellectualism expressed through reading, writing and arithmetic.

The laws of science produced by rational thinking were seen to be universally valid. As the new bourgeoisie came to identify themselves as the source of this power, it is easy to see how they then began to believe that their literary culture was also superior to oral culture and destined to be adopted universally.

The new emphasis on reason, claimed as the sole possession of the owning class, produced an awkward contradiction. Although rational thought was capable of logical analysis and exposition, it was not so useful in making judgements of value. A system of values is at the heart of all cultures. We are motivated and prioritise our actions by what we value most highly. Although it is possible to value some things in an objective, and so rational way, most things like manners, art, beauty or style, can only be evaluated intuitively.

So rational and logical thought might drive the world of science and technology very effectively, but it is intuition which is needed to make a judgement on the quality of the products of culture. As intuition was a 'lower' faculty, this contradiction threatened the theoretical justification of the dominance of the rational.

Art became central to covering up this flaw in the superiority of the rational - and the dominance of the higher faculties over the lower. Art was the place where the correct intuitive judgements were enshrined. The broader set of values, which celebrated bourgeoise wealth, masked the fact that the malignant source of that wealth was oppression. Taste is a total system of values, which ranks every part of social life. Philosophy itself had to be expressed in tasteful terms. This meant a lack of thought about emotion and silence on any direct discussions about the sufferings of exploited peoples. The relation of reason to sense, the higher faculties to the lower, became a useful analogy for speaking of class relations when it would have been too vulgar to speak directly of naked aggression and violent oppression.

On the one hand philosophy was a search for truth, a rational analysis of the human condition; on the other it was itself a cultural ritual whose function was to provide a justification for the status quo or to provide a critique with its long-term survival in mind. As a ritual, it revels in conceptual gymnastics and mind-boggling abstraction. All too often these delights become an end in themselves, which are more of a celebration of detachment than intelligence. Bourdieu (1979)496

The British Tradition of Taste and Its Justification by Philosophy

Before going on to consider the thoughts of British philosophers I should say why I should be shifting from a wide consideration of oppression to these particular thinkers. In his book *Radical Enlightenment: Philosophy and the Making of Modernity, 1650–1750* (2001) Jonathan P. Israel writes that from the 1650s on, philosophy 'burst upon the European scene' with 'terrifying force'. He describes it as 'vast turbulence shaking European civilisation to its foundation.' The process of secularisation and rationalisation seemed to be unstoppable. In contrast, contemporary philosophers don't have such influence, although they do still wield authority amongst the literary and academic scenes.

Richard Cumberland, writing in the seventeenth century was concerned at the fragility of Thomas Hobbes' system, which relied on the ability of the individual sovereign to maintain a mesmeric spectacle and gave too much power to the King alone. In keeping with the scientific tendencies of this time Cumberland suggested, in *On Natural Laws* (1672), that sovereignty had to be based on a law of nature which ordered such rights. This law was recognised as the 'common good'. It was to be administered by every citizen. The definition of citizen at this time was synonymous with the dominant class. The citizens perceived the 'common good' from two sources; from scientifically discovered principles and from their own inner sentiments; especially the sentiment of 'benevolence'. The final judgement, on the proportions in which these two sources of knowledge were applied, was ordered by God's will, also known as providence or the 'je ne sais quoi'. Filtered through the morality or conscience of the upper classes, this intuition was supposed to direct the judgements of 'good taste.'

This radical shift from the all-powerful sovereign to an all-powerful civil society directed by a code of taste, first articulated by Cumberland, was to become the basis of British civil society. It laid the foundations for the persistent compromise between the traditions of aristocratic taste and the demands of the new bourgeois 'middle' class.

Lord Shaftesbury, aka Anthony Ashley-Cooper the 3rd Earl of Shaftesbury, confirmed this profound transition in the regulation of society with his *An Inquiry Concerning Virtue*, in 1699. He followed Cumberland's argument, but his 'rhapsodic and dialogical' writing did much to widen knowledge of these radical ideas. Through the burgeoning print industry, the influence of philosophical debate spread out from the learned schools into civil society. Shaftesbury followed a triple theme:

> First: Providence or cosmic law.
>
> Second: The resulting 'beautiful order' of things, which imbues humans with...
>
> Third: The capacity to recognise and act according to that beautiful order.

This private good and interest, guided by the faculty of taste, was argued to coincide with the 'common good', So it was argued that if the ruling class followed their own interest, the 'common good' would result! Private and public interests are therefore argued to coincide. The real differences or conflicts between the private interests of the ruling class and the public interest of the people were repressed. Whatever the good citizens did in their own interest, as long as it was within the framework of good taste, would be best for all people in the end.

The beauty evident in art suggested the 'good proportions' of taste generally. It was seen to demonstrate the virtue of good taste and those who had good taste. Shaftesbury equated proportional harmonies perceived through the senses, in art, with a 'sense of proportion' about more complex matters quite abstracted from direct perception such as political matters. This kind of dubious analogy became important in the discussion of taste and judgement. It was a synthesis of ethics and aesthetics.

The Dutch immigrant to Britain Bernard Mandeville then challenged Lord Shaftesbury with his book *The Fable of the Bees or: Private Vices, Public Benefits* (1714 - 23). Mandeville impudently suggested that beauty and virtue were but 'screens for desire and appetite, masks of domination and not the greatest realities eulogised by the philosophical lord.' Mandeville even went on to point out that Shaftesbury's civil harmony and unity can only be achieved through deception and violence. 'Mandeville replaces the je ne sais quoi with a cynical I know only too well; in place of providence he puts the manipulative politician.' Both quotes Caygill (1989)52

The contradiction between the beauty of art and the violence required to coerce labour evokes the 'je ne sais quoi'. The highest beauty requires a coercion of labour to accumulate the necessary wealth. So, if we accept beauty as desirable and the highest aspect of God's will, then exploitation must be a sacrificial part of his grand scheme.

The Scottish empiricist David Hume is notable in his early work *Treatise of Human Nature* (1739) for attempting to relate reason to the senses, with its implication of class relations, without recourse to God or 'providence'. He produced a theory of social formation in which 'sympathy' for our fellows is mirrored from one person to another. The pleasure of this process indicates utility and the general abstracted result of this process results in taste, a kind of sum of the mirroring of individual sensibilities. This implied that taste was a social construction that came from the consensus of a particular class. He got little response to this work and later, in 1757 returned to the conventional 'God-given' reason for the regularity of good taste. Presumably the dominant class at this time also thought language and culture was created by God rather than evolved by humans.

David Hume's sceptical approach produced two main responses, one from Edmund Burke. Burke is famous for his later remark on 'the swinish multitude' made in his *Reflections on the French Revolution* of 1790, the book which provoked Tom Paine to write his classic, *The Rights of Man*, the following year. It is sufficient to say here that Burke restated the providential nature of the relation between the classes. The other, more influential, response was from Adam Smith.

Adam Smith, who wrote his *Wealth of Nations* in 1776, embraced the God-given 'je ne sais quoi' and pointed out that production was too complex a matter to be planned. He used the example of the labourer's coarse and rough woolen coat to illustrate the social complexity of the production of a simple item, and to argue for the self-organising nature of a free market over an unwieldy planned economy. This was also an argument for the regulation of society through taste rather than legislation. The long-term goals of human development were God's responsibility, a god who could be entrusted with progress by his infinite wisdom. He thought that 'man' should only attend to the immediate means of producing wealth rather than the longer-term ends. Of course, this gave capitalists unlimited license; apart from justifying any extreme of exploitation it was a recipe for future ecological disaster. As we are now only too well aware, a benign God has not been at the helm of the great cargo ship of capitalism.

Smith argued that a society driven to produce wealth by the contemplation of means, by the infinite mental pleasures of taste, firstly has less need of policing and state intervention as there is a general encouragement of good manners. Secondly, it replaces human desire related to finite needs with a desire limited only by imagination.

An interesting aspect of Smith was his assertion that proportion is best achieved by each class in society following their own interest. He observed that each class suffered from a lack of concern for the whole: Landowners didn't have regard for the whole because of their sloth; the bourgeoisie couldn't be responsible for the whole because of their self-interest in making profit; the working-classes lacked sufficient time and education. See Caygill (1984)96. However, if each followed its self-interest within the dictates of taste, then the result would be in balance.

The trade unions that subsequently flourished in the belly of the Empire did indeed play a positive role in rising productivity, which led to some material gain for sections of the British working-class. At the same time the framework of taste limited the unions' demands from posing a threat to the whole system. This seems to mean that the unions could not make cultural demands that could challenge the rule of judgement and taste. This idea and practice still seems to persist.

There are serious deficiencies in the market model of relating supply to demand as expounded by Smith. Just one example is the fact that market forces can mean that food tends to be exported away from famine regions.

> Adam Smith's proposition is, in fact, concerned with efficiency in meeting market demand, but it says nothing on meeting the need that has not been translated into effective demand because of lack of market based entitlement and shortage of purchasing power. Sen, (1981)

> It was Adam Smith's achievement to shift the terms of analysis from a language of rights to a language of markets. Thompson (1991

The grounds cleverly landscaped by Cumberland, Shaftesbury and Smith provided the canon for the British establishment that we have inherited. It certainly provided the theoretical justification of the deep ground of value on which the men considered in the body of this book stood.

German Aesthetics, Judgement and Feeling

As an example of how this worked out in another language area of Europe. I will briefly discuss parallel developments in Germany mainly following Howard Caygil's *Art of Judgement* (1989). In contrast to Britain, the unification of small kingdoms happened much later in German history. This was achieved through the system of 'Polizei', which called for bureaucratic administration, militarisation of social relations, the uniting of politics and economics and a directing image of metaphysical perfection. Polizei derived from the administrative innovations of Burgundy and France in the fifteenth century and entered Germany as imperial police ordinances issued by the Hapsburg court. This was only widely taken up by the territorial princes in the seventeenth century. These methods were then used to centralise the state and contain the privileges of the aristocracy and the independent cities. In this process philosophy was used to systematise the diverse pragmatic origins of the 'Polizeiwissenschaft' and to train the cadres of the bureaucracy.

Gottfried Wilhelm Leibniz, a remarkable scientist and contemporary of Hobbes, was the first German philosopher of this period. His lifelong ambition was to create a rational jurisprudence or canon of law, which was intended to be the key to a true politics of happiness. Central to this was an idea of aesthetic perfection as the metaphysical foundation of justice. This was so thoroughly established it became the consensus of the German Enlightenment until challenged by Immanuel Kant in his *Critique of Pure Reason* in 1781. Caygill (1989)126

Leibniz's idea of perfection was dynamic and reached for a harmony of freedom and justice within the Christian ethic of love. This ideal was not politically feasible so it ended up as a morality enforced under an obligation of law. In line with the Lutheran changes of the Reformation the powers of the ecclesiastical courts passed to the temporal ruler and were administered by police.

Christian Wolff developed this with an extensive and pedantically cross-referenced system from 1713 to 1721. This was dominated by the higher judgement of reason, which ordered the 'lower sensibilities'. This was carried analogously through to his political justification, in which the social realisation of perfection was via the rational sovereign who legislated the activity of the lower orders for the 'common good'. The sordid violence by which the upper class relates to the masses, by which the population is forced to conform, is disguised in the finery of metaphysical first principles and abstract analogy.

Leibniz had written in Latin and this made his work exclusive. When Martin Luther had nailed his theses to the chapel door in Wittenberg in 1517, they were printed in vernacular German. The furious and widespread debates of the Reformation that followed did much to speed the growth of both German literacy and print capitalism. The success of Protestantism was largely based on the use of the expanding vernacular print market. Christian Wolff, writing in his native language, translated a dictionary of philosophical terms and, like Lord Shaftesbury in Britain, generally made philosophical discourse much more widely available. However, the ideas he took from Leibniz lost much of their original subtlety. According to Howard Caygill his idea of perfection was a caricature of the Leibnizian original and this also goes for his metaphysics. 'Wolff transformed Leibniz's dynamic relation of unity and manifold back into a spatial relationship of part and whole ... grievously misrepresenting Leibniz's position.' Caygill (1989)126

However, the fact that art required a judgement of its perfection that stood outside of reason threatened Wolff's whole edifice. The pleasures of art are essentially intuitive and resist being reduced to a set of rules. Alexander Baumgarten produced his *Reflections on Poetry* in 1735 and was soon to become the leading Wolffian. In his *Aesthetica* of 1750 he summarises his liberal position:

- It is not necessary to tyrannise the lower faculties, but to guide them;

- In so far as it can, aesthetics will undertake this guidance;
- The aesthetician does not want to excite and confirm the corruption of the lower faculties, but to order them properly so that they do not become more corrupted through abuse, for one must avoid their misuse without suppressing a divinely bestowed talent.

This paternalism reminds me very much of the attitudes of the British philanthropists of the nineteenth-century. It is all about the wise management of the working classes as a productive resource. This is an approach that aristocrats with their knowledge of animal husbandry would have felt comfortable with.

Johann Herder then transformed Baumgarten's aesthetic into a philosophy of culture under the modern headings of psychology, art and history. He had a vision that the free exercise of human judgement would result in things being kept in proportion. In this he recaptured the insightful meaning of proportion achieved by Leibnitz from its crude interpretation by Wolff. His own solution to the 'unification of the manifold' or to the schism of reason and intuition and its implications for class division, was to propose a totalising and fundamental idea of reflection. Herder's philosophy of art, focused on sculpture, rather than poetry or painting, was published in 1778 as *Plastik*.

> On the title page of *Plastik* Herder slaps the 'epoch of beauty' in the face with a sentence from Diogenes Laertes - 'What is beauty? - that's a blindman's question.' In the text, he overturns the German Enlightenment's visual paradigm of the clear and distinct perception of a perfection in favour of a notion of perfection as 'form' or proportion which is produced and experienced through the entire economy of the senses. The distortion of this economy in favour of visual perception contributes to the creation of an ophthalmit culture which, with thousands of eyes, without feeling, without probing (tasten) hand, remains all the time in Plato's cave with no concept of any physical characteristics.
> Caygill (1989)180

Earlier, in his *Yet Another Philosophy of History* (1774) Herder writes about the 'philosophically ruled' state as being a denial of freedom: 'In its totality and in its minutest parts, it is entirely controlled by the thought of its master'. He argues that it stultifies human progress and imposes a pattern of history in which 'each man is to wear the uniform of his station in life, to be a perfect cog in a perfect machine'. Herder, quoted by Caygill (1989)183

Herder is a powerful radical thinker but he does not break out of the mind-cage of taste, although he describes it in acute detail. He is followed by Immanuel Kant who reaches the heights of finesse in elegant abstractions, discretion, diplomatic justifications and most importantly, in the consistency of his discourse.

Immanuel Kant's body of thought represents the maturing of the Enlightenment's opposition to the conventions and traditions of the landowning class and Church in feudal Europe at the end of the eighteenth century. It was a grand confluence of the British and German traditions of philosophy and it formally established the basis of the liberal ethos, which is so much a part of the ground of our thinking and common sense today, that it is invisible. The meanings of important ideas like equality, respect, freedom, human dignity, morality, individuality and rights were established and defined by Kant.

We have to keep in mind the enormity of the shift from feudal culture to appreciate the advances marked by Kant's formulations. A limited but significant proportion of the population was encouraged to think for itself, to throw off the shackles of superstition and emotional reaction and to rely on its individual reasoning powers to derive an intellectual justification for its way of living and to rationalise a morality.

> Man, in the system of nature (homo phaenomenon, animal rationale) is a being of slight importance and shares with the rest of the animals, as offspring of the earth, a common value (pretium vulgare). Although man has, in his reason, something more than they and can set his own ends, even this gives him only an extrinsic value in terms of his usefulness (pretium usus). This extrinsic value is the value of one man above another - that is, his price as a ware, that can be exchanged for these other animals, as things. But, so conceived, man still has a lower value

than the universal medium of exchange, the value of which can therefore be called pre-eminent (pretium eminens).

But man regarded as person - that is, as the subject of morally practical reason - is exalted above any price, for as such (homo noumenon) he is not to be valued as a mere means to the ends of others or even to his own ends, but as an end in himself. He possesses, in other words, a dignity (an absolute inner worth) by which he exacts respect for himself from all other rational beings in the world: he can measure himself with every other being of this kind and value himself on a footing of equality with them. Kant from his *'Doctrine of Virtue,' Part 2 of The Metaphysic of Morals* (1797)434 quoted by Seidler (1986)

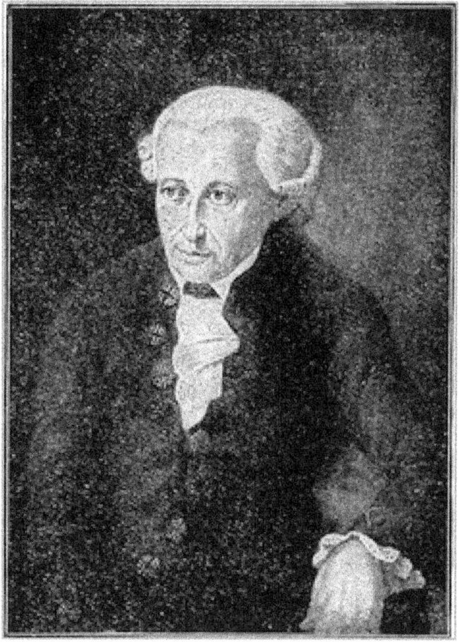

Immanuel Kant 1724 - 1804

If one could become an autonomous rational being in this way, the realm of reason was seen to offer human dignity, which was the basis of freedom. Kant's body of thought offered considerable internal logical consistency, which gave it stature, but this was achieved at cost.

The irrationality of liberal capitalism can paradoxically be traced back to Kant's rigid adherence to rationality. It is hard for us to appreciate just how integral the paradigm of 'mind over matter or the body' was to the development of capitalism. There was no way that even the sharpest brain of the era could express ideas outside the territory mapped by this fundamental worship of reason and the consequent debasement of 'matter'.

The leading role of mind over the lower faculties of the body meant that reason dominated the emotions. Kantian thought, therefore, fragmented our 'selves' between our emotional, feeling, intuitive base nature and our 'higher' faculty of reason. The emotions were not simply under the control of reason but were utterly repressed and seen as undignified. This was an extension of the necessity of all oppressor culture to repress feeling. It was Kant's achievement to embed a monumental formulation of this definition of rationality in the foundations of capitalist consciousness.

> The deep antagonism between morality as a creation of reason and our emotions, feelings, desires and needs, still organises our liberal moral consciousness. Seidler (1986)138 and 153

In his book *Kant, Respect and Injustice* Victor Seidler often refers to the limitations of Kant's perception.

> He was forced to face the realities of human dependency though he never learned to think about this systematically. p.75; It always remained difficult for Kant to consider fully social relations of inequality as proper objects of moral assessment. p.82; He does not really develop a full sense of the ways people are hurt. p.113; His moral rationalism only dimly perceived the nature of the difficulties people faced. P.161 Seidler (1986)

Remembering the model of oppression described earlier, we can see that this is likely to be another example of the emotional numbness that the majority of people of the dominant class must have to be effective in their positions of power. Seidler quotes Simone Weil who had perhaps first observed this numb characteristic of the oppressor:

> The first form of lie is covering up oppression, of flattering the oppressors. This form of lie is very common amongst honest people, who in other ways are good and sincere, but who do not realise what they are doing. Human beings are so made that the ones that do the crushing feel nothing; it is the person crushed who feels what is happening. Unless one has placed oneself on the side of the oppressed, to feel with them, one cannot understand. Weil, (1978)139

Even when the Enlightenment philosophical tradition produced its inevitable negation, Karl Marx looked at the origins of what is consumed, and the financial basis of middle-class power was clearly described, we end up with something which is still from the mind-cage of one class - which is expressed predominantly in the cultural codes and media of that class - money and book knowledge. It does not relate to the daily cultural experience of those who would be liberated. It does not empower the lives and struggle of the oppressed. Marx produced a grand narrative, which explained economic exploitation but did not find the heart of working-class liberation. The very stature of Marx's work, as a heroic monument to the intellectual negation of bourgeois culture, became used as a diversion from the development of working-class intellectual autonomy, the only really effective contradiction of oppression.

The Communist Manifesto states that the middle-class shapes the world after its own image. The Great British tradition of taste made sure that all efforts were put in place to persuade the working-classes to aspire to a pale imitation of this image instead of being proud to be themselves.

A radical analysis of the way class power was mediated through civil society was not articulated until the Italian communist Antonio Gramsci was imprisoned by Mussolini in the 1930s and worked out his theory of hegemony on sheets of toilet paper.

> Short of jeopardising their own existence as philosophers and the symbolic powers ensuing from this title... they can never carry through the breaks, which imply a practical epoché of the thesis of the existence of philosophy, that is, a denouncement of the tacit contract defining the conditions of membership in the field. Bourdieu (1979)469

Taste in Contemporary Western Culture

Pierre Bourdieu's *Distinction: A Social Critique of the Judgement of Taste* is by far the most influential work on contemporary good taste.

It was written by the French sociologist Pierre Bourdieu, using survey data from France in the late 1970s. Its analysis is widely considered as relevant to other industrialised Western states. The quotes that follow are all from this book.

Bourdieu's detailed analysis of taste is important and pioneering. Perhaps one of the most useful contributions is the graphic understanding of class oppression as having a cultural as well as economic dimension, which he expresses most clearly as a cross graph. The economic stratum a person finds themselves in is seen to equate, on average, to specific cultural preferences. This goes against the common-sense view that cultural preferences are decided by each individual.

It is important to understand the limitations of such a book rather than just be dazzled by its brilliant flights of conceptual architecture or impressed by its erudite tone. The long sentences which take our breath away in awe, can also, by the authority that this style assumes, also deny our brains the oxygen to see his limitations. Bourdieu sets out to give a cultural definition to class by using statistical data and specific examples derived from mass surveys; to give a scientific basis to the understanding of the dynamics of class identity; but we have to remember that he is writing within the context of Western academia. His analysis is achieved with a grand sweep but at the same time he is subject to the limitations of his own viewpoint as he himself admits: 'I cannot entirely ignore or defy the laws of academic or intellectual propriety.'

The danger here is that whilst he appears sympathetic he is at the same time reproducing the oppression. He indicates this in a little footnote in which he admits:

> It would have seemed somewhat cruel to quote one or another of the texts in which the 'cultivated' express their image of the 'petit-bourgeois' relation to culture and the 'perversions' of the autodidact. Bourdieu (1979)568

This shows how his text is modified within the boundaries of good taste so as not to offend. Through this we can see how extremes of class disgust have been censored from the text, as he says: 'One cannot objectify the intellectual game without putting at stake one's own stake in the game - a risk which is at once derisory and absolute.' Bourdieu (1979)163

> Distinction seeks to 'give a scientific answer to the old questions of Kant's critique of judgement, by seeking in the structure of the social classes the basis of the systems of classification which structure perception of the social world and designate the objects of aesthetic enjoyment.' Bourdieu (1979) xiii

> Whereas the ideology of charisma regards taste in legitimate culture as a gift of nature, scientific observation shows that cultural needs are the product of upbringing and education. Bourdieu (1979)1

The dominant culture is ruled by 'the ideology of charisma', which gives precedence to those who have from an early age been imbued with culture, each household being ranked in accordance to mainly aristocratic rules of precedence. Those who acquire culture by education depend for their position on the ranking conferred on them by a conscious bourgeois knowledgeability. The superior culture is one that appears to be 'natural', by birthright, rather than having been acquired artificially by study. The effect of the mode of acquisition is important. Those brought up in daily contact with ancient objects will show an apparently innate knowledge over a broader field of lifestyle than the most erudite scholar. The dominant culture pretends that it achieves a fusion of both traditions, but in reality, it is always generating conflicting claims to superiority.

Any outsider to a culture needs to know the code of that culture to get meaning and interest from it. Without understanding the code, we must stop short at the sensory qualities, or try to guess deeper meanings from our own cultural code, which may or may not share meanings in common. To this extent no work of art can be appreciated universally beyond its sensory qualities. It must be decoded.

> The encounter with a work of art is not 'love at first sight' as is generally supposed, and the act of empathy, Einfuhlung, which is the art-lover's pleasure, presupposes an act of cognition, a decoding operation, which implies the implementation of a cognitive acquirement, a cultural code. Bourdieu (1979)3

This decoding process is itself mystified and mythologised as an innate quality of those with good breeding. It is an unspoken code whose terms are learnt by familiarity. Its verbal expressions are rather general and vague terms in opposition, which only have an accurate meaning within the right context. This is necessarily so, as good taste must give a sense of the indefinable, the 'je ne sais quoi.' In this way, it protects itself from being easily picked up by the aspirational outsider.

This 'legitimate aesthetic' was argued by Kant to be superior to a 'common aesthetic' in which the pleasure to be gained is through an object's sensory pleasures, its usefulness or its meaning as a sign. In the legitimate aesthetic, the important quality is one of 'disinterestedness'. The satisfaction of the aesthete is not connected to bodily pleasures, nor to social necessities, but to an 'elective distance from the necessities of the natural and social world' which 'takes the bourgeois denial of the social world to its limit.' To put the utmost value on these qualities is to devalue ordinary life. This makes the sufferings of the oppressed seem both unimportant whilst they are at the same time necessary to do the work to produce this 'higher' realm.

The owning class aesthetic is interested in the representation and disinterested in the relation between the representation and reality. This aesthetic idea is applied to all sensory media and functions as a way of legitimating social status.

What is implied in *Distinction* is that 'the lower orders' cannot appreciate these *or any other* sophisticated pleasures. Bourdieu does not contest this, although he does protest in favour of the cultural legitimation of sensory pleasure. What is lacking is a search within the wreckage of working-class cultures for evidence of these higher appreciations of art which are not 'disinterested'. Bourdieu considers working-class culture simply what appears in his survey. He does not consider it as a repressed culture, one that exists in latent form, as if under a lid, which is outside the scope of sociological surveys, almost as a prerequisite of its existence. He does not consider the largely unwritten history of working-class culture. He says: 'It must never be forgotten that the working-class 'aesthetic' is a dominated 'aesthetic' which is constantly obliged to define itself in terms of the dominant aesthetic.' Bourdieu (1979)41. Dominated, yes, but not totally. In different areas and at different times it is less dominated. At such times, there are autonomous judgements being made that are not simply about the cultural values of the ruling classes.

'Music represents the most radical and the most absolute form of the negation of the world, which the bourgeois ethos tends to demand of all forms of art.' Bourdieu (1979)19. To anyone who knows much about the working-class traditions of music the idea that there is no appreciation of the complex or subtle abstractions of music is absurd. There is an appreciation of the same subtle relationships and qualities, but it is not put on a 'higher level,' nor does it serve the same function of 'disinterest.'

So, Bourdieu seems to be saying that working-class culture is dependent on the dominant culture and lacking in the higher qualities that the dominant culture embodies. This is nothing but the perpetuation of a central myth of oppression. On the contrary, I would say that it is owning-class culture which is organised to disguise *its fundamental lack*. It is this culture which tortuously has to perpetuate an appearance of 'civility' to cover the exploitation of labour and the abuse of human rights on which it depends. It is their culture that has grown like a cancer from ours. Most bourgeois high art is made by working people. It is working-class skills that put it all together, and it is often working-class artists who provide the innovations.

> In matters of taste, more than anywhere else, all determination is negation; and tastes are perhaps first and foremost distastes, disgust provoked by horror or visceral intolerance of the tastes of others ... which amounts to rejecting others as unnatural and therefore vicious. Aesthetic intolerance can be terribly violent. Aversion to different life-styles is perhaps one of the strongest barriers between the classes. Bourdieu (1979)56

Here Bourdieu does put his finger on the negative basis of good taste in disgust for those seen as inferior to you. Good taste is the wallpaper that covers over this class hatred. Bourdieu is immersed in and dependent on this world himself and whilst he recognises the way that popular forms of culture such as football have been transformed from participative games to spectacle, he does not look further and see what games and culture the spectators reinvent. (See for instance: Richard Turner's, *In Your Blood, Football Culture in the late 1980s and early 1990s*, Working Press, 1990).

Because working-class people have not been able to have their own cultural/intellectual apparatus it is not surprising if they do not publish a defence of their culture. Because of this repression we must look elsewhere into non-legitimate areas of culture to investigate people's appreciations and how they represent their thoughts and ideas: an example here could be the shanty houses discussed above.

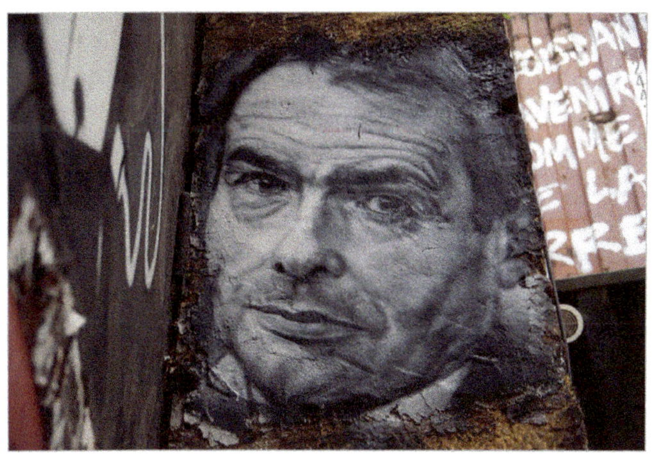

Photography by Thierry Ehrmann 2013

In Bourdieu's sociology, the lack of data due to repression is not adequately compensated for. Its replacement with stereotypes may be a true reflection of an impoverished present, but it is a block to latent becoming. He says that the dominated classes have produced no art and culture to objectify the cultural game because they are so 'imbued with a sense of cultural unworthiness' Bourdieu (1979)251. Anyone attempting to survive as a working-class artist can testify that the external barriers of exclusion are at least as great as any internal sense of cultural unworthiness.

> The educational institution succeeds in imposing cultural practices that it does not teach and does not even explicitly demand, but which belong to the attributes attached by status to the position it assigns, the qualifications it awards and the social positions to which the latter gives access. Bourdieu (1979)26

The point here, that Bourdieu seems to miss, is the way that this process is intuitively resisted by those lower-class people who attend educational institutions, even though they often seem to be unaware of the nature of the game they are entering. This resistance may not take legitimate forms and so goes unrecorded. He speaks as if the process of imposing cultural values was total, but at best it is a cultural surface over what is an altogether more profound set of values. If what is latent, buried or under the surface is not investigated, such a study will inevitably reinforce the dominant images of reality. At one point, he does have a short discussion about working-class culture in which the importance of 'an old erudite culture' is dismissed, and the existence of urban working-class art denied (see p.395). He concludes that the only option for a liberatory 'reaffirmation of cultural dignity,' therefore 'implies a submission to dominant values.' He shares here with E.P. Thompson, in his *'Customs in Common'*, unusual insight combined with a certain hopelessness about the potential of working-class culture to drive the abolition of class oppression. Neither of these great intellects has grasped the crucial fact that this attitude is itself part of the oppression which they are meant to be opposing.

Within the dominant culture there are many factions each vying for position to a greater or lesser degree. In each, there are oppositions between economic and cultural capital and between modes of acquisition of both. Radical revolts occur within the dominant culture and its institutions. What is not mentioned by Bourdieu is the way that modern hegemony contains its reversal. If hegemony is the pervasive control of the population through the many social institutions that mediate the dominant culture, then we can also observe a resistance that happens at all levels of social institutions, infiltrated as most now are by many people of working-class origins, whose respectability and middle-class identity is a brittle myth. So, the struggles within the dominant culture are not simply between internal factions of the dominant class, as Bourdieu asserts. I suspect that the dominant culture is a bubble which has absorbed so many people from 'below,' thinly disguised in good manners, that it might burst at any moment.

This is not to underestimate the immensity of the problem of dismantling the mechanisms of oppression:

> Routinely the question is that of whose opinion is voiced most frequently and most forcibly, who makes the minor ongoing decisions apparently required for the joint coordination of any joint activity, and whose passing concerns have been given the most weight. And however trivial some of these *little gains and losses* may appear to be, by *summing them all up* across the social situations in which they occur, we can see that their total effect is enormous. The expression of subordination and domination through this swarm of situational means is more than a mere tracing and symbol or ritualistic affirmation of the social hierarchy. These expressions considerably constitute the hierarchy.' E. Goffman, 'Gender Display' [paper presented at the Third International Symposium, *Female Hierarchies* at the Harry Frank Guggenheim Foundation, April 3-5 1974], quoted in Bourdieu (1979)597. Bourdieu's emphasis.

The demystification and practical deconstruction of this dominant code of manners is a historic task and one that is well within human capabilities. First, we must dare to face up to it.

Diagrams

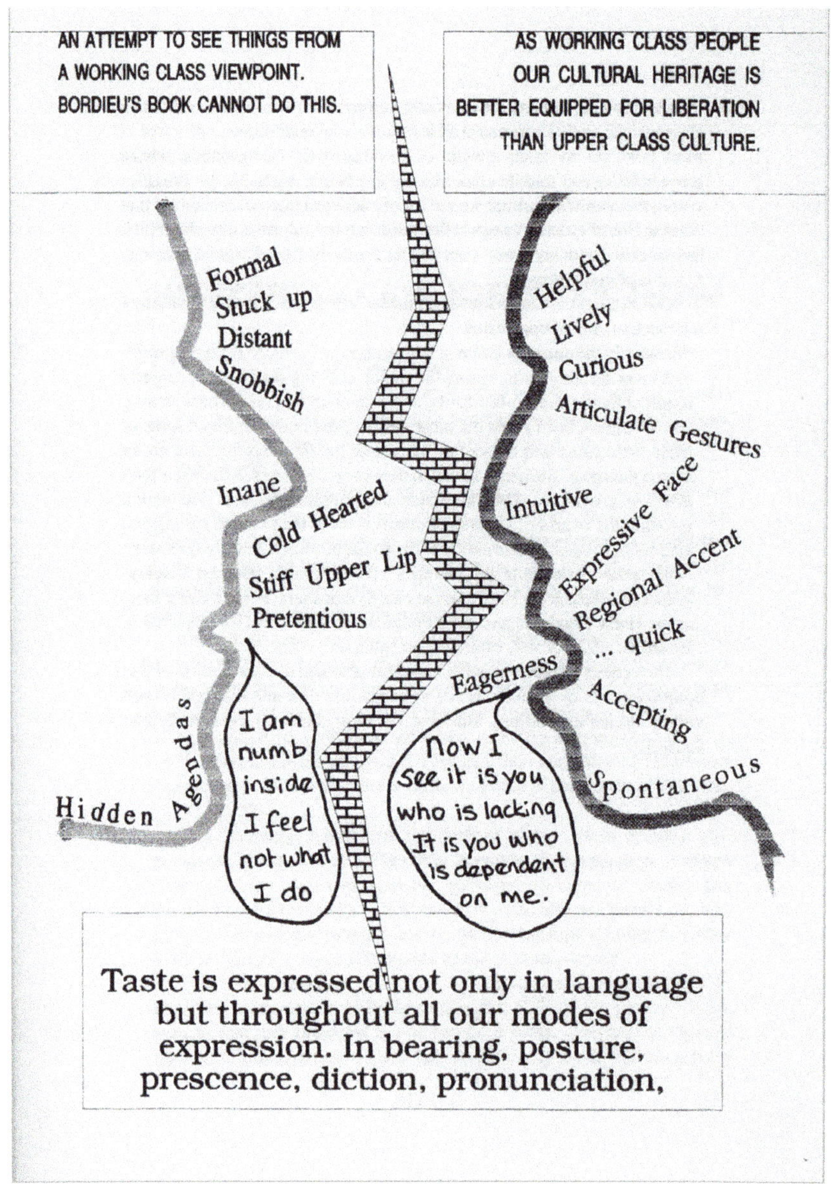
AN ATTEMPT TO SEE THINGS FROM A WORKING CLASS VIEWPOINT. BORDIEU'S BOOK CANNOT DO THIS.
AS WORKING CLASS PEOPLE OUR CULTURAL HERITAGE IS BETTER EQUIPPED FOR LIBERATION THAN UPPER CLASS CULTURE.
Formal
Stuck up
Distant
Snobbish
Inane
Cold Hearted
Stiff Upper Lip
Pretentious
Hidden Agendas
I am numb inside I feel not what I do
Helpful
Lively
Curious
Articulate Gestures
Intuitive
Expressive Face
Regional Accent
... quick
Eagerness
Accepting
Spontaneous
Now I see it is you who is lacking It is you who is dependent on me.
Taste is expressed not only in language but throughout all our modes of expression. In bearing, posture, prescence, diction, pronunciation,

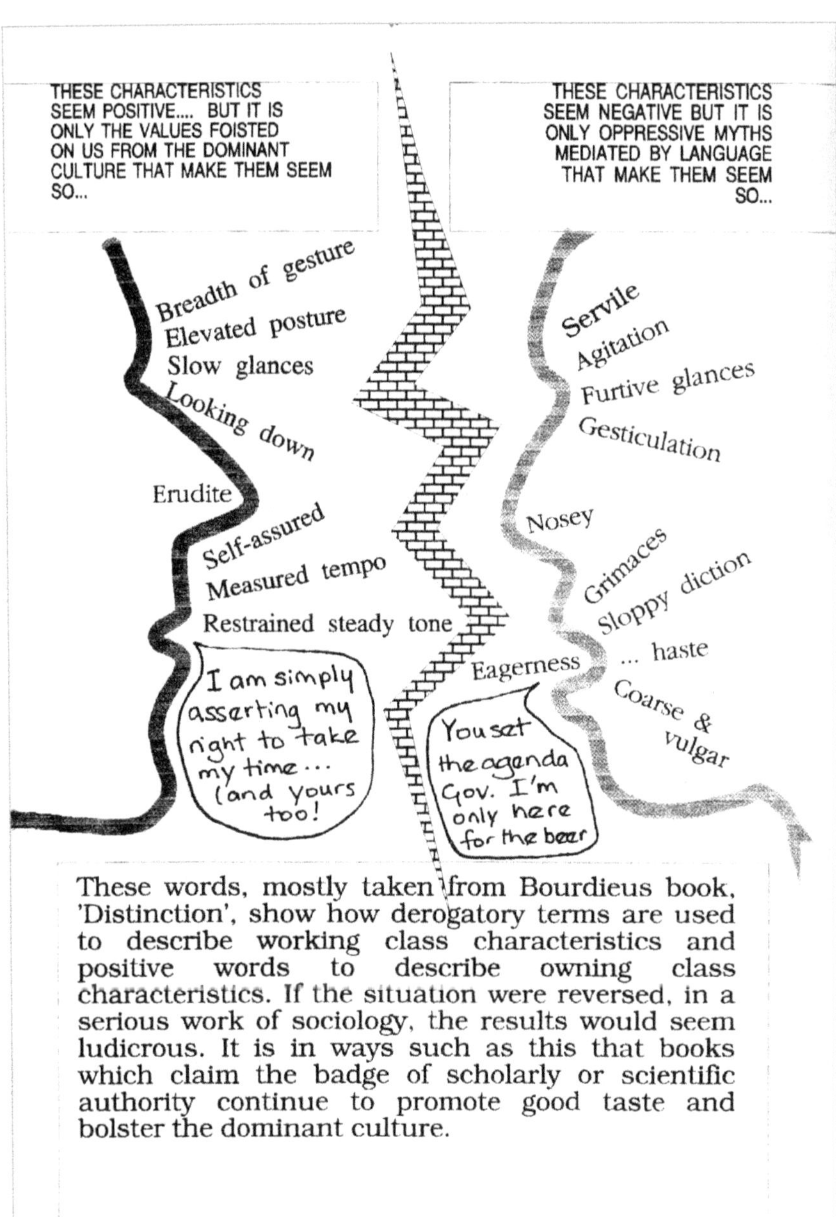

These words, mostly taken from Bourdieus book, 'Distinction', show how derogatory terms are used to describe working class characteristics and positive words to describe owning class characteristics. If the situation were reversed, in a serious work of sociology, the results would seem ludicrous. It is in ways such as this that books which claim the badge of scholarly or scientific authority continue to promote good taste and bolster the dominant culture.

DOMINANT VALUES ARE BUILT INTO OUR LANGUAGE. GIVEN BELOW ARE A FEW OF THE MOST BASIC CLASS RANKING OPPOSITIONS. THESE SUPPORT A PLETHORA OF LESSER OPPOSITIONS, EUPHEMISMS AND ALLUSIONS.

see Bourdieu p.469

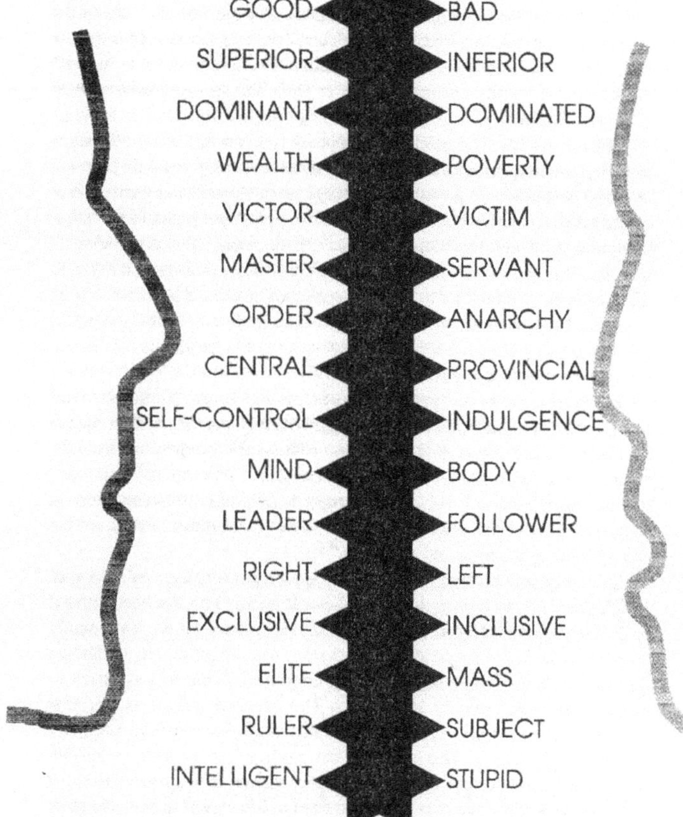

Each class and each sub-division of this class will re-use the oppositions within it to fractionalise its own group. In a dominant group there will be sub groups who are more or less dominant, who have a tendency to be left or right and so on. This multi-layering process is the order much loved by right wing politicians. A place for everyone and everyone in their place. Cosy. Secure.

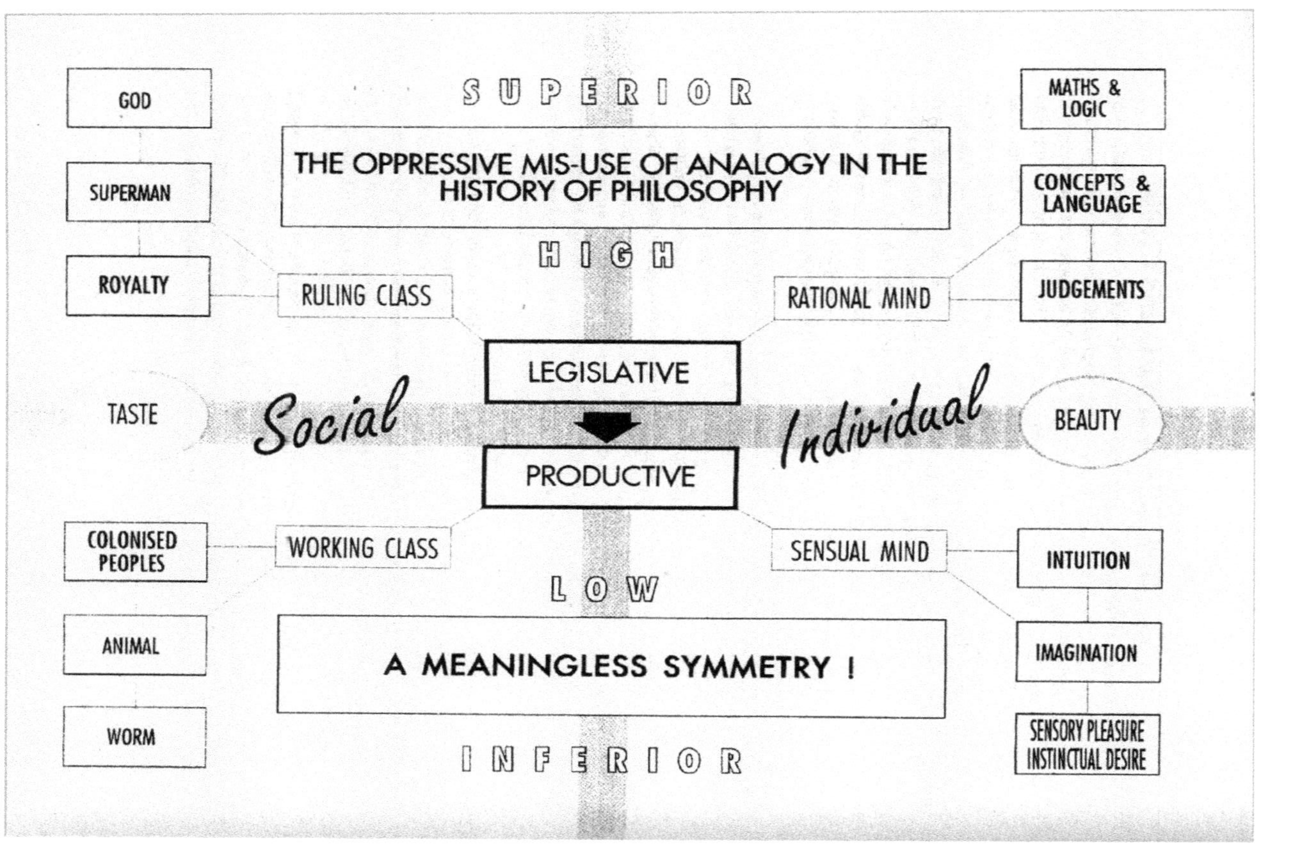
GOD
S U P E R I O R
MATHS & LOGIC
THE OPPRESSIVE MIS-USE OF ANALOGY IN THE HISTORY OF PHILOSOPHY
SUPERMAN
CONCEPTS & LANGUAGE
H I G H
ROYALTY
RULING CLASS
RATIONAL MIND
JUDGEMENTS
LEGISLATIVE
TASTE
Social
Individual
BEAUTY
PRODUCTIVE
COLONISED PEOPLES
WORKING CLASS
SENSUAL MIND
INTUITION
L O W
ANIMAL
A MEANINGLESS SYMMETRY !
IMAGINATION
WORM
SENSORY PLEASURE INSTINCTUAL DESIRE
I N F E R I O R

Conclusion

It was clear to me from my experience in the 1960s and 1970s that revolutionary politics wasn't providing effective ways of ending social injustice. As I looked for an explanation of the anger I felt so keenly about class issues, I found very little clarity of thinking around. The identity politics that emerged from that period soon showed what a dead spot existed everywhere when it came to any questions on class. Gender and Race 'awareness' has been embraced by liberal society but there was an almost complete avoidance of embracing the issue of class. I couldn't get very far thinking about it on my own and there seemed to be an invisible taboo that silenced discussion about the vile class divisions that pitted humans against each other and seemed to be at the root of all the worst excesses of human behaviour. From early on it was clear that class underpinned and unified all other 'identity politics.'

It wasn't simply a matter of politics. We'd spent a century getting almost every adult the right to vote but all this achieved was a welfare state that bureaucratised human caring and a housing situation in which working-class communities have been constantly broken up, harassed and stuck in badly-designed estates or other second-rate housing. I asked myself why working-class people hadn't called a halt to the grand scale of abuse directed against them and why middle-class people continued to be so callous and patronising in managing the society that perpetrated these mundane horrors.

The only thing I could think was that there had to be mechanisms of oppression that got at people in the process of their daily lives, as they grew up and lived their lives; mechanisms that were somehow enacted in such a way that we hadn't been able to defend ourselves.

Whilst working-class organisations had focused on the workplace, struggling for shorter hours and holidays, better pay and conditions there was something else going on in the background that had been missed; something that we hadn't fought against, because it was installed by stealth.

A general word that describes the flux of meaning and communication in our daily lives is culture. Perhaps oppression was being imposed through the ebb and flow of cultural meanings and media messages rather than just being an effect of the exploitation of our labour. It seemed to me that if we could identify the nuts and bolts of these cultural mechanisms then we could go about dismantling them. Class oppression is too easily accepted as a normal 'fact of life' rather than something imposed and vile that is newly re-imposed on each generation; something we don't have to put up with; something that degrades all humans whilst it goes unchallenged. We need to start to find out how these mechanisms work and how they can be challenged. This book is an attempt to find some clues about how class oppression has been installed and maintained through culture.

In the nineteenth-century working-class people had banded together to defend and improve work conditions with some success, but they had not defended their cultural activity so well. The importance of defending the integrity and resourcing of working-class culture does not seem to have been generally recognised. Without a well-resourced culture, any body of people lose the ability to have a sense of themselves and think critically about their situation. They lose the ability to think collectively as a social body. They do not get a sense of their own achievements on their own terms. They do not, in the main, get to tell their own stories in any medium or see themselves as key players in human history.

It seems that three interrelated things have happened to put us in this predicament. First, working-class culture was either banned outright or it was undermined and derided in a thousand ways. The audience was gradually separated from an active and integral relation with cultural production and pacified. The new urban culture moved from the Free 'n' Easies of the early Nineteenth-century to the fixed seating and blackout of the modern cinema and concert hall. Second, new urban working-class cultural forms were commercialised, professionalised and turned into self-serving commodities. Third, middle-class culture and literary knowledge had achieved such an appearance of authority that many working-class leaders were persuaded that this was a universal model which everyone should aspire to. Working-class knowledges and culture were derided and seen as worth little: middle-class culture was put on a pedestal and held up as the goal for people who wanted to 'get on' in life.

Without a culture of their own, a people are gutted. They are laid out on the slab. They can then be divided, taken apart and disposed of. What Franz Fanon said of colonial domination is reflected back in the domination of the 'natives' at home:

> The poverty of the people, national oppression and the inhibition of culture are one and the same thing. Franz Fanon, *The Wretched of the Earth,* (1961)191

That is what has happened to the majority of the population. The managers of this outrage are the middle-classes working as agents of the owning class. There has been sporadic resistance but it has never managed to link up and realise its collective power.

In this book, I've tried to get behind the civilised facade that is put up by middle-class knowledge and gather some evidence of what these cultural mechanisms of class oppression might be. The middle-class people that perpetrate the crimes of class oppression hide behind masks of respectability. They are the upright members of the community many of us have looked up to. They assure us that they are on our side and that they have 'the public interests' at heart - before they shaft us. They are the 'great and the good' - artists, architects, educators, broadcasters, and the directors and managers of our cultural and educational institutions. They manage and influence local committees and busy themselves in our affairs whilst all the while intimidating working-class people with their self-confident bluster and officious manners. Another mask that they have often hidden behind is 'socialism'. It's difficult for many working-class people to suspect a middle-class person that is apparently spouting socialist principles and doing everything for the good of the people.

I started this book off by discussing the insidious effect of William Morris's influence in the nineteenth-century. I went on to consider how the mediation of Cecil Sharp had silenced singing in vast swathes of the working classes, including in my own family. I then related the work of Clough Williams Ellis to the way we have had our ability to provide housing for ourselves excised in the twentieth century. I could have gone on to include others like Lord Reith who started the BBC:

> The pronunciation of the King's English is a sore trial to students of our own language. It is also a matter of considerable concern and irritation to ourselves ... One hears the most appalling travesties of vowel pronunciation. This is a matter in which broadcasting may be of immense assistance. John Reith, 1924

> A long talk with Lord Byng after lunch at the Athenaeum... He said I ought not to keep anyone on in the B.B.C. after being divorced, irrespective of the circumstances, which is what I have felt all along, although I was glad to have his confirmation. Reith Diaries 2-2-1927

> In six short years Sir John Reith has made himself more even than the guardian of public morals. He has become the judge of What We Ought to Want... Sir John has taught us to regard him as the last surviving Victorian father, the man who alone knows what is good for us. Helen Wilkinson M.P. Evening Standard 16-6-1931 (Thanks to Yvonne Ossei for these quotes.)

Leading writers like D.H. Lawrence, H.G. Wells, George Bernard Shaw and Aldous Huxley, who I grew up regarding as leading progressive intellectuals, were supporters of eugenics. Eugenics was created by Francis Galton who led a group who believed that society would benefit from selective breeding. The inferior classes and 'defectives' would be discouraged from breeding. The Eugenicists sought to destroy both slum dwellers and the disabled. Other distinguished modern writers feared the masses and sought to exclude them, remove their literature and deny their humanity. John Carey provides a discussion of this in his *The Intellectuals and The Masses: pride and prejudice among the literary intelligentsia, 1880 - 1939*, (1992). Such misanthropic attitudes are still lurking behind the facades of establishment institutions.

It may not be worth picking our more contemporary leaders

because nowadays the situation seems to be a lot more diffuse. The model set by the early pioneers has become a set of embedded cultural practices that is part of the normal behaviour of the ordinary middle-class managerial elite and is perpetuated through institutions like the English public-school system and the old universities. Cultural institutions like the Arts Council of England talk a lot about inclusion and creating access to the arts but we can be sure that this is not the kind of radical inclusion that is being discussed by working-class activists. (For a working-class take on inclusion see: '*Incurably Human*' by Micheline Mason, Inclusive Solutions, 2000).

Working-class people need to run their own communities, learning and cultural institutions, entertainment, welfare and everything without any middle-class management or interference. We need to do this in ways that are not directed from above but are decided by a process of local grass-root discussion and experiment. Working-class communities need to get a share of national resources that is in proportion to our numbers in the population. We need to be able to direct these resources to enrich our own lives and wellbeing. We need to make a decisive break with exclusive middle-class traditions of knowledge and culture. We need to insist that middle-class people do not manage our lives any longer.

We must also understand how the mechanisms of oppression have caused classism to be internalised in our own families and communities. The ways in which we have come to believe in the devaluation of ourselves and each other must be weeded out and refuted. This is a task of enormous historical proportions - enormous damage has been sustained in mind and body. We must ask how we are going to recover from the effects of this and stop it being passed on to the next generation.

There's bound to be variations in the details of class oppression in different cultural locations. However, I believe that something along these lines must be in effect in any advanced capitalist society as capitalism relies on class oppression. Liberal capitalism couldn't exist without an emotionally calloused middle-class to manage it, and a subdued and atomised working-class whose intellectual confidence and cultural integrity has been undermined.

This account might seem rough and ready to some readers. The only way to develop these ideas is to have a network of discussion about class run by working-class people. We need to put our thinking, research and experience together and to breach the silence that has surrounded class for so long. We need our own forums, networks and archives. Clues about how oppression works and how liberation might be achieved occasionally slip out in all media, even on mainstream TV. We need to collect all these bits and pieces and reassemble them into a form that can provide insight, inspiration and motivate dialogue in our own communities. We need new forms of research and learning which are not compliant with the emotional detachment of the literary elite.

Clearly the dominant culture is good at perpetuating itself or it would have withered long ago. An autonomous working-class culture would seriously threaten the class system. So, we cannot expect these things to fall into our laps without a severe reaction from the system. We cannot expect to get the information we need by a process of cool investigation. Oppression is embedded throughout our communities and it is going to need social convulsions to expel it. Academic knowledge sidelines emotion. A working-class rationality would embody emotion as a necessary channel through which certain crucial thinking about ending oppression can be a reached and this is one of the ways it will differ from the academic traditions.

Working-class people have achieved many things in all kinds of media from the Scottish writer James Kelman winning the Booker prize in 1994, to the worldwide success of rap music' to Caitlin Moran's Twitter feed. For some reason, this hasn't yet come together as an unstoppable force to end social injustice. We need to work out the reason this has not occurred, and plan to celebrate and discuss the work of our own brilliant artists.

The covert operation of classism under the cover of culture, what I've called the conspiracy of good taste, has pirated our history, given us false identity papers, assumed accents and an empty shell of socialism. It has denied our culture; violated our communities; invaded our minds and denied our intelligence. The conspiracy of Good Taste produces knowledge with no heart, manners with no soul, sex with no head and language without meaning. It hands out hurt and casts out healing. It is the cancer in a mother's breast. It has confused love with hate. It has taken our desire to be together and turned it out into the cold night. Good Taste is a glamorous facade which screens us from the impossibly horrific normality of the world order - like a glittering palace built on the sands of unbearable self-hatred.

In this twenty-first century, we must insist on cultural autonomy and make sure we are not palmed off by smooth-tongued officials. The working-class has been typified as stupid. In reality, it is working-class people who can best think about a new society which makes caring for each other its priority. When it comes to thinking about how to improve the quality of human relations, middle-class intelligence is calloused, blinkered and practically useless. Working-class people must help each other to recognise the quality of our own affective intelligence and put our thinking and values centre-stage in the redirection of human activities.

Stefan Szczelkun June 2001 - 2016

Bibliography

Abercrombie, Patrick. *The Preservation of Rural England*, 1926

Aronowitz, Stanley. *The Politics of Identity*, Routledge, 1992

Bailey, Peter. *Music Hall: The Business of Pleasure*, Open University Press, 1986

Bailey, Steven. *Taste: the secret meaning of things*, Faber, 1991

Barr, Ann, & Peter York. *The Official Sloane Ranger Handbook*, Ebury Press, 1983

Berneri, Marie Louise. *Journey Through Utopia*, Schocken, New York, 1971 (Orig. RKP, 1950.)

Blackwell, Trevor and Jeremy Seabrook. *A World Still to Win: the reconstruction of the post-war working-class*, Faber & Faber, 1985.

Bourdieu, Pierre. *Distinction: a social critique of the judgement of taste*, Routledge, 1984-89 (Orig. Paris, 1979)

Boyes, Georgina. *The Imagined Village: culture, ideology and the English folk revival*, Manchester U.P. 1993

Blyth, Ronald. *Akenfield*, Penguin, 1969

Briggs, Asa. ed. *William Morris: selected writings and designs*, Pelican, 1968 (orig 1962)

Alan, Carraze & Helen Oswald. *The Prisoner*, Virgin, WH Allen, 1990

Carey, John. *The Intellectuals and the Masses: pride and prejudice among the literary intelligensia, 1880-1939*, Faber and Faber, 1992

Caygil, Howard. *Art of Judgement*, Basil Blackwell, 1989

Coleman, Stephen. & Paddy O'Sullivan, eds. *William Morris & News from Nowhere*, Green Books, 1990

Common, Jack. *Fake Left*, Working Press, reprint 1992 (orig. 1933)

Cooper, Emmanuel. *People's Art: working-class art from 1750 to the present day*, Mainstream, 1994

Craik, W.W. *Central Labour College, 1909-1929*, Lawrence & Wishart, 1964

Devine, Fiona. 'Social Identities', Sociological Review, 1992

Dialogue & Humanism: The Universalist Quarterly, Vol 1. No 1, Warazawa, 1991

Dixon, Robert. *The Baumgarten Corruption: from sense to nonsense in art and philosophy*, Pluto 1995

Douglas, Mary. *Thought Styles: critical essays on good taste*, Sage, 1996

Dyos, H.J. *Victorian Suburb: a study of the growth of Camberwell*, Leicester, 1961

Farina, Richard. *Singer Songwriter Project*, Elektra, LP EKS-7299 (stereo), 1965

Faulkner, Peter. ed. *Jane Morris to Wilfred Scawen Blunt*, University of Exeter, 1986

Faulkner, Peter. *William Morris and the Idea of England*, William Morris Society, 1992

Ford, Isabella. ed. *Tom Maguire: a remembrance*, Labour Press Society, Manchester, 1895

Fried, Emanuel. *The Un-American*, Labor Arts Books, 1992

Gans, Herbert J. *Popular and High Culture: an analysis and evaluation of taste*, Basic Books, USA, 1974

Gregory, Chris. *Be Seeing You: decoding The Prisoner*, John Libbey, 1997

Hall, Peter (director), *Akenfield* (film), 1970

Hardy, Dennis. and Colin Ward, *Arcadia for All: the legacy of a makeshift landscape*, Mansell, 1984

Harker, Dave. Fakesong: *The manufacture of British folksong 1700 to the present day*, Open University Press, 1985

Harker, Dave. 'May Cecil Sharp be Praised?' History Workshop Journal, 14 #1, Autumn 1982

Hauser, Arnold. *The Social History of Art*, Vol.1, RKP, 1951

Heath, Richard. *The English Peasant*, 1893

Hewison, Robert. 'Field of Dreams', Sunday Times Colour Magazine, 3.1.93.

Hewison, Robert. *Ruskin and Oxford: the art of education*, OUP, 1996

hooks, bell. *The Will to Change: Men, Masculinity, and Love*, Washington Square Press, 2004

Howkins, Alun. *Reshaping Rural England: a social history 1850-1925*, Harper Collins Academic, 1991

Huizinga, J. *The Waning of the Middle Ages*, Penguin, 1965. (Orig. 1919)

Jackins, Harvey. *The Human Side of Human Beings: the theory of Re-evaluation Co-counselling*, Rational Island, Seattle, 1978 (second revised edition)

Jones, Sidney R. 'The Village Houses of England', The Studio, spring, 1912

Judge, Roy. 'Mary Neal and the Esperance Morris', Folk Music Journal, Vol 5, Number 5, 1989

Karpeles, Maud. *Cecil Sharp: his life and work*, originally published in 1933 in collaboration with A.H.Fox-Strangeways. Revised edition, RKP, 1967

Kirchoff, Fred. *William Morris: the construction of a male self, 1856-72*, Athens: Ohio UP, 1990

Laing, Stuart. *Representations of Working-Class Life, 1957 - 1964*, Macmillan, 1986

Lethaby, W.R. *Phillip Webb and his Work*, 1935

Levine, Lawrence W. *Highbrow Lowbrow: the emergence of cultural hierarchy in America*, Harvard, 1988

Levy, Carl ed., *Socialism and the Intelligentsia 1880-1914*, RKP, 1987

Linebaugh, Peter. *The London Hanged: crime and civil society in the eighteenth century*, Allen Lane, 1991

Loose, Jaqueline. *Duels & Duelling*, Wandsworth Libraries, 1983

Lyons, Joan. ed. *Artists' Books: a critical anthology and sourcebook*. Visual Studies Workshop, New York, 1985 - 91

Mackail, John W. *William Morris. Vols 1 & 2*, Longmans, 1899

Mais, S.P.B. *Britain Calling*, 1938

Marquand, David & Anthony Seldon. eds. *Ideas that Shaped Post-War Britain*, Fontana, 1996

Marsh, Jan. *Back to the Land: The Pastoral Influence in England from 1880 -1914*, Quartet, 1982

Marsh, Jan. *Jane and May Morris: a biographical story 1839-1938*, Pandora Press, 1986

Marsh, Jan. *Pre-Raphaelite Women: images of femininity in Pre-Raphaelite art*, Weidenfeld & Nicolson, 1987

Marwick, Arthur. *Class in the Twentieth Century*, Harvester, 1986

McAleer, Kevin. *Duelling: the cult of honour in Fin-de-Siecle Germany*, Princeton U.P. USA, 1994

Meier, Paul. *William Morris: Marxist Dreamer, Vols 1 & 2*, Hassocks, 1978

Morton, A.L. *The English Utopia*, Lawrence & Wishart, 1952

Muthesius, Stefan. *The English Terraced House*, Yale UP, 1982

Palmer, Roy. *Britain's Living Folklore*, David & Charles, 1991

Pegg, Bob. *Folk: a portrait of English traditional music, Musicians and Customs*, Wildwood, 1976

Pegg, Bob, *Rites and Riots: Folk Customs of Britain and Europe*, Blandford, 1981

Pickering, Michael, and Tony Green. eds. *Everyday Culture: Popular Song and the Vernacular Milieu*, Open University Press, 1987

Press, John & Charles Harvey. *William Morris: design and enterprise in Victorian Britain*, Manchester U.P. 1991

Reas, Paul. *Flogging a Dead Horse*, Cornerhouse, 1993

Reed, Francis. *On Common Ground*, Working Press, 1991

Richmond, Kenneth. *Culture and General Education, a Survey*, Methuen, 1963

Robinson, Lilian R. *Sex, Class & Culture*, Methuen, 1986. (Orig. Indiana UP, 1978)

Ross, Andrew. *No Respect: intellectuals and popular culture*, Routledge, 1989

Rudofsky, Bernard. *The Prodigious Builders*, Seeker & Warburg, 1977

Ruskin, John. *The Stones of Venice*, 1852

Sanderson, Michael, *Educational Opportunity and Social Change in England*, Faber & Faber, 1987

Seidler, Victor J. *Kant, Respect and Injustice: the limits of liberal moral theory*, RKP. 1986

Sen, Amartya. *Poverty & Famines*, Oxford University Press, 1981

Silverman, Jerry. *The Dirty Song Book*, Stein & Day, New York, 1985

Sharp, Cecil J. *English Folk Song: some conclusions*, Oxford University Press, 1907

Sharp correspondences, Vaughn Williams Memorial Library ms.

Shiach, Morag. *Discourse on Popular Culture: class, gender and history in cultural analysis, 1730 to the present*, Polity, 1989

Shipley, Stan. *Club Life and Socialism in Mid-Victorian London*, Journeyman, London History Workshop, 1983

Shusterman, Richard. *Pragmatic Aesthetics: living beauty, rethinking art*, Blackwell, 1992

Singing Together, BBC Broadcasts to Schools, Rhythm and Melody. BBC 1956-59

Sillitoe, Alan. *Raw Material*, WH Allen, 1972

Staffrider Journal, Vol 2, No.3 & 4, (South Africa) 1989

Steedman, Carolyn. *Landscape for a Good Woman: a story of two lives*. Virago, 1986

Swenarton, Mark. *Artisans & Architects: the Ruskinian tradition in architectural thought*, Macmillan, 1989

Szczelkun, Stefan. *Class Myths and Culture*, Working Press, 1990

Tames, Richard. *William Morris: an illustrated life 1834-1896*, Shire, 1972

Thompson, Dorothy. *The Chartists*, Temple Smith, 1984

Thompson, E.P. *William Morris: Romantic to Revolutionary*, Lawrence & Wishart,

1955

Thompson, E.P. *Customs in Common*, Merlin, 1991

Thompson, Paul. *William Morris*, Heineman, 1967

Trifit, J. (director), *Land of Lost Content*, TV film, 1989

Turner, Richard. *In Your Blood: football culture in the late '80s and early '90s*, Working Press, 1990

Vallance, Aymer. *The Life and Work of William Morris*, Studio Editions, 1986 (Orig. George Bell, 1897)

Vale, Malcolm. *War and Chivalry: Warfare and Aristocratic Culture in England, France, and Burgundy at the end of the Middle Ages*, University of Georgia Press, 1981

Walkerdine, Valerie. *Schoolgirl Fictions*, Verso, 1990

Ward, Yolanda. 'Spatial de-concentration', 1980, reprinted by *No Reservations, Housing, Space and Class Struggle*. News from Everywhere, London, 1991

Waters, Chris. *British Socialists and the Politics of Popular Culture: 1884-1914*, Manchester University Press, 1990

Weil, Simone. *Lectures on Philosophy*, Cambridge UP, 1978

Whitehead, Andrew. 'Dan Chatterton', History Workshop Journal, #22, 1984

Williams-Ellis, Clough. & J&E Eastwickenfield. *Building in Cob, Pise and Stabilised Earth*, Second edition. Country Life & Newnes, (First edition published as *Cottage Building in Cob, Pise, Chalk & Clay: a renaissance*, Country Life, 1919)

Williams-Ellis, Clough. *England and the Octopus*, 1928, reprinted Portmeirion, 1975

Williams-Ellis, Clough. 'Introduction to The Face of the Land', Yearbook of the Design and Industries Association, 1929-1930

Williams-Ellis, Clough. and John Summerson. *Architecture, Here and Now*, Thomas Nelson, 1934

Williams-Ellis, Clough. ed. *Britain and the Beast*, 1938

Williams Ellis, Clough. Untitled chapbook, Industrial Discussion Clubs Experiment, IDCE, published in the 1940s, (R.I.B.A. Library).

Williams-Ellis, Clough. *Town & Country Planning,* 1951

Williams-Ellis, Clough. *Architect Errant: an autobiography,* Constable, 1971

Williams-Ellis, Clough. *Around the World in 90 Days,* Portmeirion, 1975

Worpole, Ken. *Dockers & Detectives,* Verso, 1983

Wren, Phillip. 'Holiday Shanties in Britain: a history and analysis', m/s, thesis, Hull School of Architecture, 1981

Wright, D.G. *Popular Radicalism: the working-class experience 1780 - 1880,* Longman, 1988

Yeo, E. & S. *Popular Culture and Class Conflict: 1590 - 1914,* Harvester, 1981

Young M., & P. Wilmot. *Family & Kinship in East London,* RKP, 1957

Zandy, Janet. *Liberating Memory: our work and our working-class consciousness,* Rutgers U.P. 1995

Zatlin, Linda Gertner. *Aubrey Beardsley and Victorian Sexual Politics,* Oxford, Clarendon,

Appendix

Other 'Routine Art Co' publications relevant to this stream of thought are:

Chalet Fields of the Gower. A photographic study of Gower plotlands – plus an interview with local architect Owen Short. ISBN 9781870736114

Improvisation Rites: from John Cage's 'Song Books' to the Scratch Orchestra's 'Nature Study Notes'. Collective practices 2011 – 2017. ISBN 9781870736961

Kennington Park - birthplace of a people's democracy? Past Tense pamphlets

Agit Disco - an expanded edition with added playlists – ebook 2019

SENSE THINK ACT: a collection of exercises to describe human abilities. ISBN 9781870736121

See also:

http://stefan-szczelkun.blogspot.co.uk

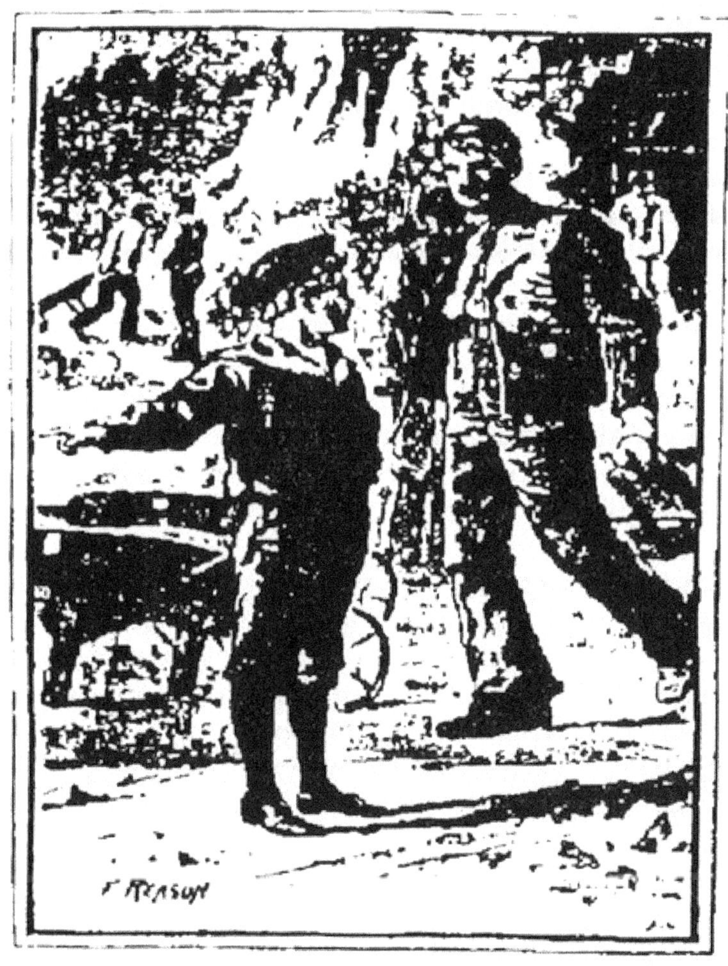

"But its *this* way for the Party's Road To Socialism you stupid bloody prole !"

www.ingramcontent.com/pod-product-compliance
Ingram Content Group UK Ltd.
Pitfield, Milton Keynes, MK11 3LW, UK
UKHW062313290726
14090UKWH00018B/1035

9 781870 736718